A Talk on Financial Education

DAVID CARLI

David Carli is not a registered investment advisor, legal or tax advisor, or a broker/dealer. All investment/financial opinions expressed by David Carli are from his personal research and experience and are intended as educational material. Although best efforts are made to ensure that all information is accurate and up to date, occasionally unintended errors and misprints may occur.

Copyright © First edition in October 2022 by David Carli.

All rights reserved. This book or any portion thereof may not be reproduced or used in any manner whatsoever without the express written permission of the publisher except for the use of brief quotations in a book review.

First Printing: 2022

ISBN: 9798359127585

Website: www.tradingwithdavid.com
E-mail: info@tradingwithdavid.com

A TALK ON FINANCIAL EDUCATION

EDITED

Caroline Winter
caroline.winter4@hotmail.com

CONTENTS

Introduction – About the Author   1

Chapter 1 – Introduction   3

Chapter 2 – Pursuit of wealth   6

Chapter 3 – Making savings pay off   10

Chapter 4 – The eighth wonder of the world   13

Chapter 5 – Assets and Liabilities   17

Chapter 6 – Debts   21

Chapter 7 – The first mistake to avoid   24

Chapter 8 – Trading and Investing   27

Chapter 9 – Dispel a myth   31

Chapter 10 – Stocks   34

Chapter 11 – Bonds   40

Chapter 12 – Investment funds   44

Chapter 13 – ETPs   47

Chapter 14 – ETFs   49

Chapter 15 – Classification of ETFs   54

Chapter 16 – ETCs   57

Chapter 17 – Criteria for choosing ETFs and ETCs 61

Chapter 18 – How to choose an ETF, example 1 67

Chapter 19 – How to choose an ETF, example 2 73

Chapter 20 – How to choose an ETC, example 3 77

Chapter 21 – Creating a portfolio 80

Chapter 22 – Some portfolio types 85

Chapter 23 – Conclusion of the financial journey 91

About the Author
Introduction

My journey in the investment and trading world started shortly after I graduated from the University of Pisa, Italy. I then travelled to New York City USA., where I attended exclusive courses by Steve Nison who introduced the western world to the art of the Japanese candlestick as a tool for analysing market trends and investment decisions.

I have been working as a full-time trader and an independent financial analyst since 2007 hence I established Trading with David as a niche investment service with the primary focus on FX markets and commodities. During that time, I collaborated with reputable financial trading services and investment magazines. And from 2012 -2013 I worked as a hedge fund manager for an Italian Bank boutique. In 2018, I began providing market analysis and trading ideas for a major European commodity investment company up to this date.

I published several trading and investment books to pass on my knowledge and expertise on how to analyse the financial market correctly and have the odds on your side to become a profitable trader. My approach is based on low-risk investment strategies across all markets to achieve a balanced asset allocation through diversification and risk management.

I have several other books for those who wish to learn more about certain aspects of trading such as Forex,

Commodities, Options, Spread Trading, and Stocks so you can see how I approach other markets. Through educational channels, I coach independent investors on my personal trading strategies and how to apply them in different market conditions.

You can find out more about my educational library on https://tradingwithdavid.com to develop an extraordinary edge to your trading and investments plan with a deep understanding of the macro environment, along with advanced technical analysis and risk management they are designed to build or improve your trading skills.

A TALK ON FINANCIAL EDUCATION

INTRODUCTION
CHAPTER 1

I will start right off with a cold definition. Financial education "is a process through which consumers, savers, and investors improve their understanding of financial products and the concepts behind them, and through instruction, information, and advice develop attitudes and knowledge to understand the risks and opportunities for making informed choices, where to receive support or help in making those choices, and what actions to take to improve their status and level of protection" (OECD).

More simply, "Financial education is the ability to understand and apply different financial skills effectively, including personal financial management, budgeting, and investing."

I'm Italian and I live in Italy. The latest analysis carried out by Standard and Poor's and the World Bank is merciless. Italy is 63rd in the world for the population's knowledge of financial mechanisms.

It's not just a question of knowing how to make an investment or exploit a financial instrument to try to get rich, it is actually about the basic knowledge needed to manage savings. This implies, in fact, that most Italians are completely at the mercy of financial institutions (banks).

According to one survey, in Italy, only 37% of

adults have at least a minimal knowledge of finance. The financial literacy rate is 68% in Canada, 67% in the UK, 66% in Germany, 64% in Australia, 57% in the US, 52% in France and 49% in Spain. Scandinavian countries have the best rates in the world, as, all together they boast 71% of the population having finance knowledge at a basic level.

The above analysis concerns concepts such as numeracy, risk diversification, inflation and interest. It was not a question, therefore, of investigating concepts of high finance, but of competence regarding the most basic economic notions that are nevertheless important in everyday life. Basic concepts that should be part of the common vocabulary of an average citizen. And yet, this is not the case. But why is it important to know how to deal with concepts such as inflation and interest?

The dossier explains that while those with a certain financial literacy are able to make informed and reasoned decisions about their savings, investments and spending, people without the most basic financial concepts are incapable of handling even the simplest of financial tasks. This means they risk making serious mistakes with dramatic consequences.

Financial ignorance can bring with it truly significant costs. In fact, consumers who fail to understand concepts such as compound interest, inflation or risk diversification often find themselves spending more on unnecessary financial transactions, thereby accumulating debt.

"Education is the great engine of personal development. It is through education that a farmer's daughter can become a doctor, a miner's son a mine boss, or a child born into a poor family the President of a great nation. Not what we are given, but the ability to make the most of what we have is what distinguishes one person

from another." (Nelson Mandela)

A few months ago, I read an article that reported on a survey conducted in Italy in the pre-Covid period. More than 36.6% of those interviewed did not have sufficient resources to face more than two months without income and two families out of ten did not have the financial means to face one month without income. Three in ten of the households surveyed would find it difficult to cope with a medium-sized unexpected expense and 35% said they felt anxious about their financial situation.

Now, I don't know what the situation in other countries is, the percentages are probably lower in many places, but what I do know is that there are still too many families that could live a better life if they had the knowledge to do so. Instead, they struggle to make ends meet or have to get into debt with banks.

I'm not here to tell you what to do, I'm neither a financial advisor nor a family banker. I have simply accumulated my experience and knowledge, derived from reading several books written by those more knowledgeable than me. Here, I have created a sort of path that will lead anyone who wants to change their relationship with money to greater knowledge and awareness of how to do so.

Although some of the changes outlined here will seem impossible to implement into daily life, you must believe me that having conviction and determination will enable you to achieve the goal you have set for yourself. Nothing you will read in the next "chapters" will be impossible.

But enough of the chatter, it's time to get started. I wish you all a happy reading and hope this advice may benefit you.

A TALK ON FINANCIAL EDUCATION

PURSUIT OF WEALTH
CHAPTER 2

One of the books that helped change my life the most and that I loved reading right away is "**The Richest Man in Babylon**" by George S. Clason. I want to be clear from the outset: any book I recommend on this educational journey of mine, should you decide to buy it, will not earn me a penny. On the other hand, I'm sure that you will receive great benefits from reading them.

There is one sentence that turned a switch on in my consciousness. It is a sentence during a dialogue between two friends, Bansir and Kobbi in the first chapter: "*the reason we never found wealth is because we never looked for it*". At the time, I was not yet trading for a living. Partly because I wasn't able to make consistent gains, month after month, but also partly because my capital was modest.

I worked as a dealer, selling stamps and coin collectables. Things weren't going badly for me, but the salary I was getting was barely enough to make ends meet. And all I knew how to do was complain about the fact that "*I worked all the time, but there was never anything left in my pocket*". That sentence had thrown reality in my face. The only thing I had to complain about was my immobility. I didn't like my situation, yet I wasn't doing anything to change it.

This is what I also see in friends and acquaintances

who struggle with their salaries and with making ends meet. These people live a life they don't like and passively accept it as if there were no solution to their condition.

"How's work?"

"Tell me about it, in this economy, I don't even know if the money will last until my next paycheck."

"Why don't you think about how to improve your financial situation?"

"Eh, you're quick to talk, you're rich (???), I break my back all day and don't have a dime, what do you want me to think about."

Apart from the fact that I'm not rich, this dialogue reveals the kind of mentality of most (if not all) those who have financial problems or who have to break their backs in order to not have them and who accept this condition, not even thinking about it, not even looking for a solution to their problems.

Going back to the sentence in the dialogue at the beginning of the book, "*the reason your situation hasn't changed is because you've never tried to change it.*" The first thing you must do is change your "loser" mentality and set your goal firmly in mind. You must be willing to make any sacrifices to achieve it. If you don't feel a desire to change, then your situation will not change. Luck should be sought, not passively waited for.

At this point, it is up to you to get started. The first step to take once you receive your paycheck is to pay yourself first, before anything else. Such a statement may sound strange, how can we pay ourselves? "*A portion of everything you earn is yours to keep. Set a reasonable portion of your earnings, making sure it is not less than the tenth part, and keep it. Modify your other expenses if necessary but first, keep that amount.*"

But how, you will say. I can't make ends meet and now I should also take 10% off my salary? It seems absurd. That's what I thought.

"What each of us calls necessary expenses will always increase to equal our income unless we do something about it. Don't confuse necessary expenses with your desires [...] There are often some expenses, now taken for granted, which can be wisely reduced or eliminated."

I did something that very, very few people do. I drew up a family budget. I created a table where every month I entered the income and expenses in their various items, even the smallest and most insignificant. At the end of the month, I had the whole account, all my income and all my expenses.

The first month my budget was close to zero, that is, the expenses represented practically the total income. So I circled all the items that weren't essential and that, if I didn't make those expenditures, I could still live comfortably, paying rent, utilities, food, and everything else that was essential.

Those circled items accounted for a good chunk of my outings. Giving them up wasn't easy and, more importantly, it wasn't enjoyable. There were dinners at pizzerias, TV subscriptions... in this way the quality of my life would have gone down a lot. But if I wanted to change things, if I wanted the wealth that would enable me to afford even the superfluous, I had to make that sacrifice.

The first months were hard, very hard. Then, slowly, as time went by, I began to get used to it and after that, it didn't weigh on me as much. On the contrary, seeing my capital grow every month by 10% of my income gave me a great feeling of satisfaction. For the first time in my life, I was saving money and that made me feel good.

So, keep a family budget where you enter all the items in and out. Evaluate all your expenses well and eliminate those that are unnecessary, even if they generate pleasure and you find it hard to give them up. Take that 10%, every month, and put it away in savings.

Most people underestimate the importance of drawing up a family budget, but I assure you that if you do, you will develop a different mindset that will help you achieve your financial goals.

This is the first step you need to take. Do it now, not tomorrow or a week from now. Now.

"Like a tree, wealth grows from a tiny seed. The first coin you save will be the seed from which your tree of wealth will grow. The sooner you plant your seed, the sooner the tree will grow. And the more faithfully you nurture and water that tree with substantial savings, the sooner you will enjoy, satisfied, its shade."

Making savings pay off
Chapter 3

At this point, after explaining the first step you have to take, there will be some of you who will think "*I'm fifty, what do you want me to do at this age to save a few pennies a month, I better enjoy my money while I can.*"

If I may say so myself, fifty is not old (otherwise I would be old myself, being fifty-one). Nowadays, it is a fact that life prospects have increased. And if you feel old, you have children, grandchildren, associations worthy of receiving donations... You can still do good for those you love (and that isn't nothing).

On the matter of two pennies... "*If you had kept aside a tenth of everything you earn, how much would you have gotten in ten years?*" Algamish the moneylender asked. "*How much I make in a year,*" replied young Arkad. I think you will all have come to the same conclusion, after all, mathematics is not an opinion. With a salary of € 1,500 per month, after ten years you will have € 18,000 (for the moment, let's leave out the inflation component). This is already a big step forward compared to ten years earlier, and all with just the first step I have laid out (and a small sacrifice).

However, Arkad's answer is half true. "*If you want to become rich, your savings must yield and these annuities must yield in turn to give you the abundance you crave.*"

This alludes to the second step you have to take. You have to make your savings make more money. This is where a very powerful, basic concept emerges that I will explain in more detail in the next "chapter".

"A man's wealth is not in the coins he possesses, but in the income he builds."

The worst thing you can do is leave money sitting idle in your checking account. The economic uncertainty of the last few years, especially with Covid-19 and lockdowns, has caused people to take the decision to not make any kind of investments, preferring to deposit money in their checking account, which they deem safer. What these people are doing is ignoring the fact that with each passing day that money loses value due to inflation.

Inflation, in economics, indicates a generalized and continuous growth of prices over time. It is a fundamental indicator because the level of prices conditions the purchasing power of families, the general trend of the economy and the orientation of the monetary policies of the central banks.

All over the world, especially in the United States, inflation is increasing due to the economic stimulus implemented to counteract the problems caused by Covid-19 and this leads to higher prices and less purchasing power of one's money.

That 18,000 euros saved in ten years, with an inflation of 2% per year, will eventually be worth as much as 16,150 euros ten years earlier. You will have lost 1,850 euros just from the passage of time and inflation. And that's because you paid 150 euros a month. If you had paid in the full 18,000 euros initially, the depreciation would have been greater (about 3,300 euros). Don't you think this is a bad way to manage your savings?

Certainly, it is understandable that most savers regard the financial markets, in particular the stock market, quite negatively. This derives not only from a lack of acquaintance with the markets and their dynamics but also from media "terrorism" by tv and newspapers. After all, the collapse of the American S&P500 index by 6% in a single day is more newsworthy than the growth of the same index by an average of 9.8% per year in the last twenty years.

There are big misunderstandings related to even the simplest concepts about finance. There are very simple and intuitive instruments that most people ignore that I will explain in the second part of this journey.

The most fundamental concept for personal growth and for financial growth is that you have to make your savings pay off. These must generate money which in turn must generate more money.

And this is the second step you need to take in your journey.

A TALK ON FINANCIAL EDUCATION

The eighth wonder of the world

Chapter 4

When investing, time is a factor of the utmost importance. I personally believe that an investment should have a minimum term of 15 years. Only in the long term can you make the most of the most important mathematical formula in a person's life: compound interest.

"Compound interest is the eighth wonder of the world. He who understands it, earns it; he who doesn't, pays for it." (Albert Einstein)

Compound interest occurs when the interest earned on an investment is reinvested and added to the initial capital, thereby generating further interest.

To better understand the advantage of using compound interest, I will compare two 15-year investments, both of $ 10,000 with an annual return of 5%. The first has a simple rate, the second instead has a compound one.

The person who invested his $ 10,000 at a simple rate of 5% will receive an annuity of $ 500 per year, so at maturity, the total reached will be $ 10,000 + ($ 500 x 15) = $ 17,500.

The person who invested his $ 10,000 at a

compound rate of 5% will have $ 20,789.28 after 15 years. For the calculation, you can use an online calculator like this one (https://www.thecalculatorsite.com/finance/calculators/compoundinterestcalculator.php). Below, you can see the result.

Year	Interest	Total Interest	Balance
0	--	--	$10,000.00
1	$500.00	$500.00	$10,500.00
2	$525.00	$1,025.00	$11,025.00
3	$551.25	$1,576.25	$11,576.25
4	$578.81	$2,155.06	$12,155.06
5	$607.75	$2,762.82	$12,762.82
6	$638.14	$3,400.96	$13,400.96
7	$670.05	$4,071.00	$14,071.00
8	$703.55	$4,774.55	$14,774.55
9	$738.73	$5,513.28	$15,513.28
10	$775.66	$6,288.95	$16,288.95
11	$814.45	$7,103.39	$17,103.39
12	$855.17	$7,958.56	$17,958.56
13	$897.93	$8,856.49	$18,856.49
14	$942.82	$9,799.32	$19,799.32
15	$989.97	$10,789.28	$20,789.28

Figure 1 - Simple interest

Thus, compound interest would have generated a net gain that was about 45% higher than that obtained with simple interest. And as the years go by, this difference increases more and more. After 30 years, simple interest will have continued to yield an income of $ 500 per year for a total investment of $ 25,000. Compound interest, on the other hand, will have increased the principal to $ 43,219.42.

Therefore, you can see how important compound

interest is to long-term investments, and how fundamental it is to start saving as soon as possible, without procrastinating. Phrases like "*yes then I will...*", "*now I think about it...*", "*in a few years I will...*" have only one purpose, to make you lose money.

This is why I make this appeal so much to young people. Save up, even just $ 50 or $ 100 a month will make all the difference in the world. Initially, it will be little but when you get to my age, you will bless the day you started doing it. Look below to see how much you can earn, even when starting from scratch and paying $ 100 a month for 15 years.

Year	Deposits	Interest	Total Deposits	Total Interest	Balance
0	$0.00	--	$0.00	--	$0.00
1	$1,200.00	$27.89	$1,200.00	$27.89	$1,227.89
2	$1,200.00	$90.71	$2,400.00	$118.59	$2,518.59
3	$1,200.00	$156.74	$3,600.00	$275.33	$3,875.33
4	$1,200.00	$226.15	$4,800.00	$501.49	$5,301.49
5	$1,200.00	$299.12	$6,000.00	$800.61	$6,800.61
6	$1,200.00	$375.82	$7,200.00	$1,176.43	$8,376.43
7	$1,200.00	$456.44	$8,400.00	$1,632.87	$10,032.87
8	$1,200.00	$541.19	$9,600.00	$2,174.05	$11,774.05
9	$1,200.00	$630.27	$10,800.00	$2,804.32	$13,604.32
10	$1,200.00	$723.91	$12,000.00	$3,528.23	$15,528.23
11	$1,200.00	$822.34	$13,200.00	$4,350.57	$17,550.57
12	$1,200.00	$925.81	$14,400.00	$5,276.37	$19,676.37
13	$1,200.00	$1,034.57	$15,600.00	$6,310.94	$21,910.94
14	$1,200.00	$1,148.89	$16,800.00	$7,459.83	$24,259.83
15	$1,200.00	$1,269.06	$18,000.00	$8,728.89	$26,728.89

Figure 2 - Compound interest

Warren Buffett, one of the richest men in the world with assets of over $90 billion, started saving from the age of 11. I hope this spurs some of you to start saving (if you haven't already). You will learn how to do this in part 2 of this journey.

Another advantage of compound interest is that leaving your gains invested means they will not generate taxes to be paid for as long as they are not cashed (at maturity of the investment). Well, you may say, sooner or later anyway, I have to pay the taxes, what difference does it make? Very true, but by not paying them immediately, you will have more money to add to your capital which is generating more interest and believe me, this is not a small thing.

Compound interest is a great "invention." Alas, it is also used in reverse against you by banks when you apply for a loan or a mortgage. The instalments of a loan, for the first few years, will be composed almost entirely by interest and very little by capital, meaning that the following year, you will find yourself with practically the same amount of debt. This can be ruinous for you, especially if you have taken out a mortgage.

It is important, therefore, to know the potential that compound interest has, and how you can use it to your advantage, whilst being aware of the ways it can be used against you.

A TALK ON FINANCIAL EDUCATION

Assets and Liabilities
Chapter 5

Before continuing this journey, I would like to complete this first part by discussing a book written by Robert Kiyosaki. There are few people who have not read his "**Rich Dad, Poor Dad**" (click on the title to buy it on Amazon) in which the author recounts his childhood in which he explains how he lived with two fathers.

His natural father was a man who has completed his studies, specialized and then became a professor, yet always had financial problems (poor father). His father's best friend, on the other hand, despite not having completed any studies, became one of the richest men in Hawaii (rich father).

The most important thing is not money, but education. Those who are pliant and open-minded get rich despite changes. Intelligence solves problems and produces money. In the long run,

"it doesn't matter how much money you make, but how much you are able to keep, and for how long you keep it for."

The number one rule, and the only rule, is to distinguish between assets and liabilities.

In the world, there are three types of categories of people from an economic point of view: the poor, the middle class, the rich. The interesting thing is that this difference is not (only) due to how much money each individual earns but where this money flows, i.e., cashflow. There can be lawyers who earn ten times as much as a clerk and still have problems.

Cashflow is very simple to build, at the bottom you put two boxes, which are filled with assets (left) and liabilities (right). At the top, we put two other boxes, one for income, one for expenses. As shown below.

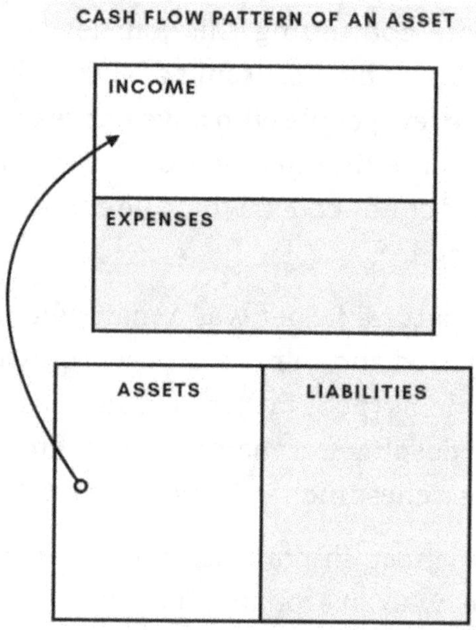

CASH FLOW PATTERN OF AN ASSET

INCOME	
EXPENSES	

ASSETS	LIABILITIES

Figure 3 - Cashflow

Before we go any further, let's take a closer look at the individual entries:

- <u>Cashflow</u>, the direction in which money flows.
- <u>Income</u>, money earned. In most cases, this comes from a job.
- <u>Expenses</u>, the money we spend to support ourselves,

our family and everything we own.

- <u>Assets</u>, anything that contributes to our income (bonds, stocks, real estate, etc.).
- <u>Liabilities</u>, whatever increases expenses instead of generating income.

In the diagram, the flow of money is represented with arrows. So, the top part is a profit and loss account, the bottom part is a balance sheet.

- <u>The cashflow of a poor person</u> is as follows: money comes into the Income box from work. From there it goes down to Expenses: taxes, food, rent, clothing, transportation, and so on.
- <u>The cashflow of a middle-class person</u> is this: money comes into the Income box from work. From there it flows down to the expenses seen above. But that's not the end of it, in fact, there are also liabilities: the mortgage for the house you own, consumer loans, credit cards.
- <u>The cashflow of a rich person</u> instead has arrows that go in an upward direction: he has assets (bonds, stocks, real estate, intellectual property) that produce income such as interest, dividends, rental income, royalties.

This is why having more money is not enough, because the cashflow model you have in your head will be reinforced. For example, if you have more money and start living in a bigger house your expenses will also increase. Therefore, a change in mindset is necessary.

The "secret" to getting rich is to be able to distinguish whether what we are buying is an asset or a liability. It may happen that an object, such as a house, can be an asset or a liability depending on the use we make of it. It is an asset if it is rented and, after deducting expenses and taxes, generates an income. It is a liability when it is, for instance, the house in which we live and which doesn't generate income but rather only expenses.

So, in conclusion, the message Kiyosaki sends with his book is not to live a moderate life, free of vices. What matters is timing. Every vice becomes accessible if it comes from earning your assets, whereas it isn't if it comes from your work.

What matters is changing your mindset. You have to realise that it is money that has to work for you, not you for your money.

"Focus on spending your money on assets, not liabilities, until the money you earn from your assets is even higher than your salary."

And when those assets generate enough income to cover all your expenses, you will have become financially independent and have gained the most valuable asset: free time.

DEBTS
Chapter 6

Let me give you a brief summary of what you have seen so far. If you want to improve your financial condition, and with it the quality of your life, it is essential that you change your mindset. With your salary, before everything else, you have to pay yourself for at least one-tenth of your income. After that, you need to make your money produce money. This is done by investing in activities that generate income (assets) and not liabilities.

Now, before I move on and develop the second step (making savings work), I want to deal with a thorny subject. Certainly not all of you, but there will be some people who, for various reasons, have taken on debt which will surely be a source of concern.

Firstly, I should start by distinguishing the types of debt:

- *Good debt*
- *Bad debt*

The latter is what most people contract and is called "<u>bad</u>" because it's set up to spend money on something that doesn't produce income, i.e., liabilities (car, vacation, latest iPhone model, etc.).

"<u>Good</u>" debt, on the other hand, is created to buy

an asset which in turn will generate income. Of course, there will be interest to pay but if the income from the asset is at least equal to the amount to be repaid plus interest, this will result in free money received (and an asset which will produce income even after the debt has been repaid).

Unfortunately, modern society is based on appearances which offer the means to squander money on useless things that gratify us in the immediate moment. So, many people, especially young people, are influenced to spend through channels (like Instagram and YouTube) and pushed to live in a constant desire to purchase useless things. Too many people go into debt to satisfy the desire for "liabilities".

Credit cards are the best way to incur these debts. How many of you are having trouble repaying what you have spent on your credit cards?

I have a few friends who are struggling with debt. I myself have been in debt in the past. I was young and not inclined to wisdom. I used to buy lots and collections with the promise of paying for them once I sold them but when that happened, instead of fulfilling my promise I spent that money on other collections or worse yet, on myself.

A solution to the problem of debt comes to us from Dabasir the camel merchant (from "The Richest Man in Babylon"). It is not an easy method to put into practice and requires sacrifice and willpower. But if your desire is to get out of debt, you will succeed.

Dabasir wrote on five clay tablets describing the way in which he repaid his debts. The plan has three goals:

- <u>It must ensure future prosperity</u>. So, a tenth of the income must be set aside and saved.
- <u>Seven-tenths will be allocated to expenses</u> (housing,

food, utilities, etc.).

- <u>Each month, two-tenths of the earnings must be divided equally towards paying your debts</u>. In this way, over time, the debts will be paid off.

This is the plan, described by Dabasir himself as "<u>invaluable</u>". What you need to do is to draw up a family budget. Eliminate all items that are not necessary for living, even if it costs you to do so. Make sure that your expenses don't exceed seven-tenths of your total income. With the remaining three-tenths, one will be allocated to you and saved, the other two will be used to honour your debts.

Being able to repay a part of your debt contracted each month will give you much more serenity and will help you to improve the quality of your life even if you have to give up things that previously gave you pleasure (if for a few years, your smartphone isn't the latest model on the market, believe me, you can survive this).

I myself, after a few years of dastardly choices, put this plan in place to get rid of my debts; and if you are thinking that you will never be able with your income to do as I did, the answer is provided by Dabasir himself,

"where there is determination, a way can be found."

A TALK ON FINANCIAL EDUCATION

THE FIRST MISTAKE TO AVOID

CHAPTER 7

Having looked at the differences between assets and liabilities, I now want to focus on the former, or rather, on investments, particularly financial ones. It must be said that there is a lot of distrust surrounding the stock exchange and investments. Partly fed, as I have already written, by newspapers and TV that report only particularly negative news.

Savers are thus inclined to perceive financial markets as dangerous, thereby influencing them into keeping their savings in their current account and seeing their purchasing power eroded by inflation every year. This means that their wealth doesn't increase and their situation doesn't change.

Many of you will have a family member, friend or acquaintance who has bought stocks and lost part of their capital. This may have led you to compare the stock market to gambling, considering it unethical. The reality, however, is very different from what you think.

This is why it is very important to have a proper financial education. It should be a taught subject, just like literature and mathematics, right from primary school. It is crucial that children be taught to understand the meaning of saving and investing.

But before I explain how you can make your savings pay off, I want to talk to you about a mistake that this very lack of knowledge could lead you to make. Trusting advice given to you by the wrong people.

"The gold in a man's purse must be guarded with great care, or it will be lost."

Advice, as a former colleague of mine once said, has two qualities: it is useful and it is free. This all depends on the person giving the advice, though.

The young Arkad invested his first savings by giving the gold to Azmur, the brick-maker, so that on his next journey he might purchase, on his own account, rare jewels from the Phoenicians. Thus, when he returned to Babylon, they would sell them by dividing the profit.

Unfortunately for Arkad, the investment went bad. The Phoenicians sold Azmur worthless pieces of glass that had the appearance of gems, and his gold was lost. *"Every fool must learn, why trust the knowledge of a brickmaker's jewels? Would you perhaps go to the baker and ask for stars? No, if you had the ability to think you would go to the astrologer."*

These days, there are many brick makers posing as financial experts.

A phrase I found on an Italian website and turned into my motto (a soft way of saying I "stole" it) goes like this,

"no one outside of you is worthy of handling your money because only you know the effort you put in to get it."

In a few words, this is the essence of investing. You alone know how much effort it cost you to earn your salary every month. You alone know the sacrifice of saving 10% of that salary. The worst choice you can make is to trust people who only care about their own gains.

You must decide for yourselves how to invest your money. "*Of course,*" you will say, "*I don't understand anything about investments, I would end up losing my savings anyway*". That's why it's important to have a proper financial education. This doesn't mean being an economist who graduated with top marks from some prestigious university. It means knowing the financial markets (don't worry, they don't bite nor do they don't transmit any nasty viruses). What is important is knowing what instruments to use and being aware of what you are doing.

I created this journey to give you a basic financial education, to give you the stimulus to put into practice some aspects and have the desire to deepen others. What you have read and what you will read is not a commercial technique to sell you some courses or financial services for a fee. I don't have any to sell and I'm not interested in doing so. I wouldn't recommend anything that would put your savings at risk.

My goal, and desire, is to make people become more aware of their finances and above all, more responsible in the management of the money that they have earned over time. Deciding to delegate these responsibilities to others (banks) is very expensive and not always, as you will see later, particularly fruitful, as often their results are not much better than what you could do independently with simple tools. You will learn to use said tools if you continue this educational journey.

So, forget about the many gurus hanging around on the internet and for once, bet on yourself.

TRADING AND INVESTING
CHAPTER 8

Another brief excursus in order to elucidate an aspect that very often becomes a source of incomprehension: the difference between trading and investing. Trading and investing are often used as synonyms, but they refer to two totally different practices. I am a trader, what I do is speculate on financial markets. I work specifically with Forex (currencies) and commodities (such as wheat, coffee and oil) and my operations have a duration ranging from a few weeks to a few months. So, I work in the medium term.

There are traders who work in the short term, with operations lasting up to a few days. There are those who do day trading, opening and closing an operation on the same day. And scalpers, who open and close many operations of very short duration (from a handful of seconds to a couple of minutes) that incur minimal gains, but that at the end of the day form an altogether nice sum.

Every trader has a different personality and a type of trading that suits him better than any other. However, all these ways of trading have one principle in common: they all try to take advantage of price movements, whether up or down. This is what the trader (and therefore me) does.

What interests the trader, therefore, is that the price of their financial instrument moves: in fact, the more it moves, the more there is an opportunity to have a rendering. But the more it moves, the more the risk of losing increases, obviously. For this reason, there are very important elements that the trader uses in his analysis, such as volume and volatility.

Volume is the number of stocks, bonds or contracts that have been traded during a given time period (e.g., in an hour, day, or week). Volatility is a measure of how much the prices or returns of an asset or financial product have moved over time.

The trader does not generally intend to buy or sell an instrument itself, but only to speculate on a price trend, earning if his predictions turn out to be correct. He, therefore, focuses more on the technical aspects of the financial instrument (be it stocks, bonds or futures) than on long-term opportunities.

Trading requires you to devote a lot of time to it, spending many hours in front of the monitor to check price trends and look for opportunities to open a trade. This amount of time is greater the smaller the time perspective of the operation is.

Trading is a real entrepreneurial activity that requires excellent knowledge of financial markets and lots of experience.

Investing, however, is a strategy that aims to increase capital over time and/or get an income. It means having a long-term perspective (at least 10 years).

An investor maintains his positions throughout the investment period, both during market upturns and downturns, rebalancing and correcting them when necessary (however, this doesn't occur frequently), until he reaches his investment objective.

He is not interested in predicting how prices will behave in the short term, but rather is concerned with understanding the fundamentals of the company or instrument in which he has invested. Therefore, the investor will possess that instrument materially, whether these are actions, bonds or quotas of a fund.

Investors are required to spend little time on their investments precisely because of their long-term view, meaning they don't have to check performance at every moment. I don't spend more than two hours a month checking, evaluating and possibly changing my investment portfolio.

Compared to trading, investing has an additional advantage: the ability to diversify your savings more. A diversified investment portfolio has positions in many companies, sectors and geographic areas: diversity helps you seize more opportunities and, above all, enables you to decrease the risk of the impact of some bad investment on savings.

For example, stocks are great in times of economic growth, commodities are good for guarding against rising inflation, and gold and some currencies, such as the Swiss franc and Japanese yen, are useful in times of recession. All together, they can create a balanced and protected portfolio.

Investing means defining a multi-year plan to reach one's life and investment goals (supplementing one's pension, having an annuity, paying for one's children's college, etc.), and requires respecting it over time whilst trying to reduce risks as much as possible.

Ultimately, although both refer to the financial markets, trading and investing are two different worlds, with totally different characteristics and objectives. Trading is earning from speculation; investing is obtaining a periodic return from one or more financial instruments.

A TALK ON FINANCIAL EDUCATION

DISPEL A MYTH

CHAPTER 9

Before I go any further, I want to explain what the stock market really is, as simply and clearly as possible.

Most people have a wrong perception of the Stock Exchange and financial markets. Partly derived from the news they hear on TV or read in the newspapers (which is always negative) and partly from the experiences they hear of relatives and friends who have "played" in the stock market and lost money.

Unfortunately, lack of financial education leads these people to see stock markets as something negative, leading them to often compare investing to gambling. But the reality is very different. Investing in shares does not mean trying to improvise as traders, it actually requires knowledge of the markets and the dynamics that move them. Analyses of the balance sheets and of future strategies of the company must be made... these are all things that require competence and experience – skills that most people do not have.

You need to understand that buying a stock without the slightest knowledge of the stock market, simply because a friend has advised you to, perhaps someone who works in the bank or because you read on the internet how simple and easy it is to earn with stocks, has little chance of earning with trading. The fault does not lie with the stock market, that is 'bad' and 'ugly'. The fault lies in the presumption of those who believed themselves smarter than others when instead they have only shown themselves to be silly and superficial.

For instance, this is a bit like the sea. The sea is not dangerous for those who are familiar with it; those who know how to behave in it and what to do and not to do in different situations. But for those who are careless and ignore even the most elementary rules of navigation, these people risk serious consequences, entirely of their own making.

For this reason, I do not recommend investing in individual stocks unless you have enough knowledge and experience of the stock market to make those types of investments. If you do have this knowledge, then you certainly don't need to read this educational path of mine.

To understand how difficult is to invest in stocks, I will tell you an anecdote.

Warren Buffett made a bet in 2009. He made a bet with some of the biggest and most prominent investment funds that they would not be able, over a ten-year period, to beat the performance of the S&P 500. In 2019, Buffet won the bet.

For this reason, my (and not only my) advice is to invest in financial instruments that replicate the performance of stock market indices. Without stress and high expenses, you will get a higher result than funds do (at least most of them) without you needing to have the same knowledge possessed by a fund manager.

"*What if the stock market crashes? I still lose my money.*"

There have always been economic crises with collapses in stock markets, and there always will be. You must keep in mind the time frame of your investment: you are not trading, but investing your savings for 20, 30 or 50 years (this depends on you and, first of all, your age).

Those who, in January 2000, had invested in the American index S&P 500, today would have an increased capital of about 250% (or even a little more, if I remember correctly). And this is despite the bursting of the speculative bubble of internet stocks in 2000, the attack on the Twin Towers in 2001, the bankruptcy of Lehman Brothers in 2008 (with the S&P 500 that came to half its value) and the pandemic in 2020. Each time, the index has then recovered what was lost, reaching new highs (this includes after the crash of 1929).

The main problem of those who invest their savings, even correctly, is psychological. Faced with a collapse, they panic and perhaps give in to fear, closing their investments early and with a loss. This involves them ignoring the objective of their investment and its time perspective (duration).

I myself allocate a portion of my earnings from being a trader to the investment plan I have studied. I am able to see, before my eyes, the benefits I gain from it, even though there have been years when I saw my capital decrease.

So do not fear the stock market. If you respect it and use it in the right way, it will be a valuable ally to your financial growth.

STOCKS

CHAPTER 10

The first thing I discussed is how you don't have to trade with your savings, but rather, that you should invest them. "*But how is this possible – you are a trader yet you are telling us we don't have to trade?*" Exactly! Not that trading is wrong, but it does require a lot of experience and knowledge of the market you are working with (stocks, bonds, currencies, commodities), as well as a lot of discipline, and this is something that you don't have right now, it would only lead you to lose money.

If you like or are curious about trading, then nobody is forbidding you from studying, reading books (even better if they're mine), consulting websites, following capable traders and analysts and beginning to learn about the markets you are interested in. Trading on demo platforms (many brokers allow you to open a demo account) and making operations with virtual money. In this way you will begin to build the experience necessary to perform this activity without having to risk losing money. But definitely do not do it with your own savings, not to begin with. If you are a beginner, you will not be able to trade successfully, not for a long time.

So, from now on, when I talk about buying a particular financial instrument I will always be referring to investing.

When you think of the stock market, generally, you are probably thinking about stocks. Buying a stock (such as Amazon) and then selling it at a higher price seems very easy, but in reality, for those of you who have little knowledge of this, it almost always leads you into losing part of your savings.

This is because investing in stocks requires a lot of experience in financial analysis. You have to make a deep analysis of the balance sheets and future prospects of the company you are going to invest in. What's more, this may not be enough to avoid losses.

Every year, Warren Buffett spends tens of thousands of dollars in reports on the companies he is interested in investing in and yet he is not exempt from making mistakes. Think now of yourself, with none (or little) experience, and without reports that give you the kind of information Buffett has – how likely are you to earn from your investments? (Not including classic beginner's luck, which does not count).

When you invest, you should rightly look at the gains you could make, but you should not forget the risk you will incur to get that gain either. Investing on one stock means putting all your savings into one company. But what if that company has problems that you aren't aware of, and that shortly thereafter cause it to fail? What would happen to your savings? They would vanish like mist in the sun.

History is full of famous cases of important companies that, for one reason or another, have failed: Enron, Lehman Brothers and these days, Evergrande (just to name a few). Think if you had invested your savings on one of those companies, you would have lost all or almost all your money.

So, investing on one company, even if it is famous and important, like Amazon, is not a good choice. The right way to go about investing is to diversify. Invest on multiple companies so that if even one has a problem, it will no longer affect 100% of your investment but only a small percentage. You will soon see how you can go about doing this.

After this long introduction and explanation of why you shouldn't invest on individual stocks, let's now take a look at what a stock is.

A stock is the smallest part into which the capital of a corporation is divided. The holder of the share (shareholder), therefore, owns a "little piece" of the company, with all the rights and obligations that this entails. The joint-stock company, on the other hand, finances its business by issuing and placing shares.

It is not necessarily that a corporation is listed on the stock exchange. So, while it will be easy to buy and sell shares of listed companies (just go to the bank or open an account with one of the many online brokers), it is more difficult to do so with companies not listed on the stock exchange. You will have to agree privately with the shareholders of the company on the price at which to buy and sell them.

Stock has two prices:

- <u>nominal price</u>, the value of the share when it is issued;
- <u>market price</u>, once issued at par, a share can be traded and the price will be determined by the meeting of supply and demand.

Among the rights conferred on the purchaser of shares is that of participating in the division of profits in the form of dividends. It may happen, however, that one year the company does not distribute profits, in order to reinvest them in the company itself. In this case, the undistributed profits is reflected in the value of the stock.

On the day of the ex-dividend, the share price opens with a lower price than the day before because it is lowered by the value of the dividend. If the company does not distribute profits (i.e., dividends), the share price will not change (in practice, the dividend remains embedded in the share price).

In order to receive dividends, it is sufficient to be in possession of the company's shares at the time of payment, i.e., when the dividend is detached. In order to be entitled to a share of the profits, it is necessary to buy the stock a certain number of days before the actual payment: for example, Italian shares must be bought at least 3 days before.

So, there are two ways to make money by buying stocks:

- *Through the collection of dividends*
- *Through the return generated by the shares*

There are several types of action, the main ones being:

1. <u>Ordinary shares</u>: These are the classic publicly traded shares that represent a company's share of capital and make up the majority of shares issued.
2. <u>Preferred shares</u>: These usually do not carry voting rights, and holders of these types of shares are generally repaid a fixed, or higher, dividend than holders of common stock.
3. <u>Savings shares</u>: These are shares that can only be issued by companies that have listed common stock and have the following characteristics:
   - are preferred in the distribution of profits, which is generally 5% of the nominal value of the shares;
   - shall take precedence over the capital in the event of liquidation of the company;

- it is not possible to exercise voting rights at ordinary and extraordinary shareholders' meetings.

The only cost you have when you buy stocks is the commission charged by the bank or broker when you buy and sell.

When you consult the quotation of stock on the main daily newspapers, you are confronted with a series of useful data for a quick evaluation of the action.

- <u>the price</u>, the price at which the stock closed the last session (i.e., stock exchange day);
- <u>the variation today in a number of points</u>, i.e., the variation in the price of the share compared to the closing of the previous day;
- <u>today's variation in percentage terms</u>, i.e., the variation in percentage terms that the share has recorded, compared to the close of the previous day;
- <u>the price range of the last 52 weeks</u>, represents the price range (minimum/maximum) in which the share has moved over the last year;
- <u>the daily exchanged volume</u> indicates the number of shares exchanged during the last session.

As we have seen, there are two ways to earn with stocks, through dividend income and through the yield generated by the stock. As for the latter, you can earn by buying a stock and then reselling it once the price has increased or through short selling.

Short selling consists in selling shares without being in possession of them (thanks to the loan of the securities by banks or brokers), and then buying them back later when the price has fallen.

It must be said, however, that this strategy is not suitable for a long-term investment as a company tends to improve and grow over time. Short selling is used exclusively by traders who speculate on the fall of stock in the short term.

BONDS

Chapter 11

Bonds are probably the most widely used financial instrument by investors as they are considered safer than others, such as the stock market.

What is a bond?

A bond is a security debt issued by an issuing company to finance an asset, with a commitment to paying interest (a coupon) over the life of the loan and to return the entire principal to the buyer at maturity.

In even simpler terms, by purchasing a bond, an investor lends money to the issuing company, which undertakes to pay him an annual amount of interest and to return the money lent at maturity.

Bonds are issued in order to raise capital for investment, directly from savers at more advantageous conditions than bank loans. The advantage for the issuing company derives from interest rates that are usually lower than those it would be obliged to pay by applying for a bank loan with the same maturity.

The two main aspects for the investor are:

- *Receiving the payment of an annual interest called "coupon";*

- *Obtaining the repayment of the invested capital at maturity.*

Based on the coupon, a bond is classified as:

- **with a fixed coupon**, the amount of interest is fixed for the entire duration of the bond;
- **with a variable coupon**, the amount of interest varies from year to year on the basis of a reference parameter that may be financial (such as EURIBOR) or real (such as inflation);
- **without coupons**, they do not pay interest. They are characterised by the fact that the issue price is always lower than the redemption price. They are known as Zero Coupons.

A bond has three prices:

- **issue price**, which is the price paid by the investor at the time of subscription and is equal to 100;
- **purchase price**: this is the price the investor pays to purchase the bond on the market. It can be one of two types: "clean price" if it represents only the value of the capital, "dirty price" if, in addition to the value of the capital, the accrual is also added, i.e., the part of the interest accrued from the last detachment of the coupon until the time of purchase;
- **redemption price**, is the price at which the bond is redeemed and, subject to exceptions, is equal to 100.

Bonds have a minimum denomination, i.e., a minimum trading amount. Generally, it is 1000 euros (but you might happen to come across higher denominations). This means that, for example, I cannot buy bonds for 58,600 euro, or 58,000 or 59,000. It may seem a trifle, but I assure you that for those who diversify their investment on several issuers, it is not a factor that should be underestimated. In the prospectus, you can find this information alongside all the characteristics of the bond.

As mentioned, bonds are probably the most widely used instrument by investors, given the many advantages they offer. They are:

- **Low risk**, limited to the possible default of the issuing company and a few other aspects that you will see later on;
- **Ductile**, they lend themselves very well to any type of investment and financial planning;
- **Clear**, as they allow you to know, even before purchasing, what their performance will be;
- **Give peace of mind**, since they are not affected by any collapse of other financial markets, as they always pay the coupon, regardless of anything else;
- **They don't need much time spent on them**.

But like all things, bonds also have cons. The biggest risks you face by buying a bond are:

- **Default**: there is a risk that the issuing company will be unable to meet its commitment and pay the periodic coupons and/or repay the principal. This is rare but not impossible (Argentina, Lehman Brothers, Greece...). It is important to check the rating, i.e., the judgement issued by private companies (Moody's, Standard & Poor's, Fitch, etc.) on the ability of the bond issuer to meet its obligations, before proceeding with the purchase.
- **Currency**: there is a risk if you do not invest in bonds in your own currency, that the yield will be eroded by the exchange rate. Attractive coupons can lead to unpleasant surprises, so you should consider your purchase carefully. If your currency appreciates significantly against the currency of the bond, you risk losing a lot of value on your investment.
- **Inflation**: there is a risk that the currency depreciation will be greater than the bond's yield. In other words, that the inflation rate will be higher than the annual interest offered by the bond. This is certainly the

current case in the United States. One solution may be to invest in bonds indexed to the principal, i.e., that at maturity return the principal revalued by the inflation accrued from the date of accrual (i.e., the day from which interest begins to accrue) to the maturity date.

- **Interest rates**: there is a relationship between interest rates and bond prices. When interest rates rise, consequently the price of bonds decreases. Conversely, when interest rates fall, the price of bonds rise. However, there is only a risk if you sell a bond before maturity. At maturity, as you have seen, the redemption price will always be 100.
- **Coupon distribution**: this is not a risk but a flaw that bonds have. Distributing coupons does not allow for the yield to accumulate, that is, for it to be added to the price of the bond. You have to be the one to do this, reinvesting what you receive in the same bond. However, this is not always possible, such as when your coupon is lower than the minimum denomination. And you have seen how important compound interest is to investment.

As I have said, bonds are a very ductile financial instrument that lends themselves well to various financial objectives, the degree of risk, the time perspective or the protection of savings from inflation. They can also be included in more complex strategies, in addition to other financial instruments, as you will see in the penultimate chapter concerning zero-coupon bonds.

INVESTMENT FUNDS

CHAPTER 12

Investments fund another important instrument amongst the most well-known by beginner savers. Omitting academic definitions that are difficult to understand, in order to comprehend investment funds, try thinking of a large piggy bank where the money of both small and large savers goes.

The management of this "piggy bank" is entrusted to an Asset Management Company (AMC) that offers the advantages of a professional investment service to all savers who otherwise, having a small capital at their disposal or lacking the necessary skills, could not afford it. The decision of what to buy with the money in that "piggy bank" depends on the investment objective of the fund.

In practice, an investor delegates the choice of how to invest their savings to the fund manager (and this conflicts with my motto).

Investment funds, therefore, are a form of asset management that collects investors' savings, which are then managed by the Asset Management Company (AMC) through a professional manager, as a single asset, in financial assets such as bonds or shares, with the aim of outperforming the market. This is why it is said to have "active" management.

Active management provides a professional manager with a margin of discretion, which allows him to vary the composition of a fund according to his own expectations, so as to favour financial assets which should be more likely to offer above-average returns, thus allowing the fund to perform better than the reference market.

In reality, this isn't as nice as you would think. Investment funds should have the advantage of diversifying investments on more financial assets, thereby reducing risks, on top of being managed by professionals. But because of their "active" management, they have very high costs. Generally, they have:

- entry fees, at the time of purchase of the share;
- management fees, i.e., recurring costs (usually annual) linked to the administration of the fund;
- performance fees, proportional to certain results achieved by the instrument;
- exit fees, at the time of the sale of the share.

These fees are not small either, I assure you (considered that it will be you, with your commissions, that will be paying the salaries of the managers of the fund). Also, although these funds are managed by professionals who, through just active management of the patrimony, aim to beat the market, their performance is nonetheless very often inferior.

Statistics show that a fund that outperforms its benchmark one year rarely succeeds in doing so the following year, thus demonstrating that that outperformance was the result of chance rather than the manager's skill.

However, you should know that there are funds that claim to implement active portfolio management while in reality, they adopt passive management (which I will explain later). In these cases, you pay fees to the fund manager when you shouldn't be.

Another "defect" would be the lack of transparency since the saver cannot know in detail or in a timely manner the financial products that constitute the assets of the fund. The data that are disseminated, in fact, are always late and often incomplete.

Unlike other instruments, investment funds have no price limit. When placing your order, you only need to enter the quantity you are interested in and that corresponds to the amount you want to invest. All buy/sell transactions entered will be settled on the basis of the end-of-day value (NAV, Net Asset Value). Therefore, investment funds are bought and sold "in the dark". Only the day after the operation will you know the price paid or received.

If you have a pressing need for the money you have invested into funds, then these are not for you, because the time it takes to disinvest is long. Due to a complex mechanism of communication, it can take up to 15 days before you will have access to the money in your bank account.

Given the many flaws that investment funds have, you may be wondering why banks and promoters insist so much on you subscribing to them. The answer is simple, every year, investment funds guarantee lavish commissions that pay, as aforementioned, manager salaries, also serving to fatten the budgets of banks.

So why pay high fees every year if a fund is not able to perform better than the benchmark and, indeed, often performs worse?

If you thought that investment funds were the right thing for you, don't be disheartened. There is, in fact, a financial product that keeps all the advantages of funds intact and is able to turn their disadvantages into advantages.

ETPs

Chapter 13

This financial product is called an ETP.

To deal with ETPs in their entirety, I would need to write a whole other book. In this path, which aims to give you greater knowledge and awareness of financial markets and how to manage your savings, I will explain only the main aspects of ETP's, referring you to more in-depth reading (there are many books in all languages) for a more complete knowledge of this valuable tool. Even if on a practical level, the notions you find in this path are sufficient, further reading will deepen your understanding.

I just want to specify, for those who do not know the English language well, that ETPs is the plural of ETP. The same goes for all the other acronyms you will see below.

So, what is an ETP?

An ETP, Exchange Traded Product, is a type of investment that is characterised by passively replicating a reference benchmark and being listed in real-time on a regulated market. The benchmark is a reference parameter, generally a stock exchange index (e.g., the FTSEmib, the Dax or the Dow Jones).

That ETPs adopt passive strategies means that they aim to replicate the performance of the reference benchmark, not to outperform it like an investment fund. For example, an ETP on the Nikkei index replicates the performance of the Japanese stock index. Hence, the risk-return profile will also be in line with that of the benchmark.

Within the ETPs are:

- **ETFs**, Exchange Traded Funds, are special investment funds that passively replicate a reference benchmark.
- **ETNs**, Exchange Traded Notes, are financial instruments with no maturity date that are issued by banks against direct investments by the issuer in the reference benchmark, which generally consists of an index (equity, bond or monetary), or in derivative contracts on the same benchmark.

A particular type of ETNs is constituted by **ETCs**, Exchange Traded Commodities, which are characterized by investing and replicating the performance of one or more commodities.

In the next sections, you will see ETFs and ETCs explained in a little more detail, albeit in a simple way, and how to use them to create your ideal investment portfolio.

ETFs

Chapter 14

An Exchange Traded Fund, or more commonly ETF, is a tool in the financial investment world that helps you choose how to invest in the stock markets and beyond. It is a kind of investment fund but it is constructed differently and has many more advantages.

The peculiarity of ETFs, as you already know, is that they adopt passive strategies. They are created by independent external companies and then issued on the market, like any other listed company. Therefore, performance, but also the risk/return ratio, are perfectly in line with that of the reference benchmark.

So, passive management of ETFs is already an advantage over investment funds that too often underperform the benchmark.

Before seeing the advantages of investing in ETFs, let me show you concretely with an example of what an ETF is. The most famous and important stock index in the world is the S&P 500. This index includes the 500 largest capitalised American companies such as Apple, Amazon, Coca-Cola, IBM, Microsoft, Netflix, Walt Disney and many other famous US companies. This index is constantly updated so that it always contains the 500 best companies. If one loses value, it is replaced with another.

Capitalization is defined as the number of shares issued by a company multiplied by the value of the share. For example, Amazon has issued 506.44 million shares which multiplied by their value ($3,425.52 at the time of writing this text) gives a capitalization of $1,734,820,348,800 (just under $2,000 billion). Obviously, while the number of outstanding shares remains unchanged (those are, regardless of who buys and sells them), the price changes from day to day and with it the capitalization of the company, i.e., in the example of Amazon.

SPY is the ticker (i.e., the identification code) of the ETF on the S&P500. What does SPY do? It simply replicates the performance of the US index. So, if the S&P500 gains 2%, SPY gains 2%; if the S&P500 loses 0.8% SPY loses 0.8%. However, although it is very rare, a tracking error can occur, i.e., a deviation between the actual performance of the ETF and the performance of the reference benchmark. This can have a number of implications, such as high costs affecting the performance of the ETF.

So basically, what is SPY? You have to see SPY as a large basket within which all 500 companies listed on the S&P500 reside. Buying a share of the SPY ETF means investing in all of the top 500 U.S. companies. The same goes for any other ETF that replicates a benchmark (SPY's benchmark is the S&P 500 index).

We must also distinguish equity ETFs, which replicate a stock index (such as the Frankfurt Dax or the Japanese Nikkei) with sectors (such as banking, real estate, pharmaceuticals, etc.) that are monetary, bond, structured. In short, you can invest and construct your portfolio however you believe is best. Moreover, you will see in more detail how you can do this later. ETFs also differ in the type of replication: physical or synthetic. I will cover this aspect with ETCs.

ETFs are generally very liquid instruments, meaning it's easy to find a buyer or seller. And that makes the risk of having to sell with no buyer's next to nil, which could cause the price of the ETF to fall. However, sometimes you may come across ETFs that have a low average daily trade value, which means they are not very liquid and not ideal to include in your portfolio. But don't worry, there are so many ETFs listed in the various exchanges from which you can invest, you will surely find the most suitable for your investment.

Now I will list the other benefits of investing in ETFs.

1. **Easy to trade**. ETFs are listed on the Stock Exchange and like common shares, they can be purchased on the platform of any regulated broker (or at least in a bank), immediately and at perfectly known prices. Moreover, the minimum tradable lot is one share. So, even from the point of view of the amount to invest, it is really accessible to everyone. These characteristics reflect the great flexibility of this instrument, which makes it suitable both for small private investors, who can access the main market indices without having to buy all the securities present in the basket and for larger institutional investors.

2. **Transparency**. At any time, the investor may know the market price of any ETF and its composition. All the data relating to the ETF are public and can be consulted both on the website of the Exchange where the ETF is listed and on that of the issuing company. So before investing your savings you can properly inform yourself about the ETF you intend to buy.

3. **Security**. What is invested in ETFs is separated from the capital of the company that issues and manages them. So, the money is still returned to the investor even if the issuing company goes bankrupt. To be fair, this is also a feature of investment funds.

4. **Diversification**. Diversification is the golden rule for all investors who want to reduce the risks of their investments. As you have seen, investing in SPY (or on any other ETF) does not mean investing in one stock but on a basket of stocks. One advantage of ETFs is that they allow small savers to access markets that would otherwise be difficult to access, such as bonds from Asian countries or equities from emerging countries. You can thus decide to buy several ETFs, thereby further diversifying your investment and considerably reducing your risk.

5. **Low risk**. By diversifying you have seen that you reduce the risks. By investing in SPY for example, even if one of the companies in the ETF were to go bankrupt, this would affect "on average" 0.2% of your investment. I write "on average" because stocks within the ETF don't all weigh the same. For example, SPY consists of 6.56% Apple stock, 5.39% Microsoft stock, 4.38% Amazon stock, 1.90% Tesla stock, and so on (percentages are purely indicative, as the S&P 500 index tends to rebalance periodically and consequently so does SPY).

6. **Low fees**. ETFs, unlike normal mutual funds, do not have entry, exit and performance fees. You will pay only a small commission to purchase and sell (depending on the broker and might range from a few euros to fifteen for banking institutes). The reason for the smaller costs is found, as you have seen, in the "passive" nature of the management of ETFs that, therefore, do not need huge resources relegated to research and detailed analysis of the choice of best stocks, that is, those that need to beat and exceed the benchmark.

7. **Shorter disinvestment times**. Unlike investment funds, the time it takes to receive your money is much shorter. Once you sell the units of the ETF(s), the money will immediately become available in your account. If you use an online broker, you have to

request the transfer to your account, which usually takes a maximum of 48 hours.

If you are wondering why your bank or financial promoter has never suggested you invest in ETFs, the answer is very simple: ETFs do not generate to banks any profit. Never forget that banks will always look out for their own interests, never yours. They have everything to gain if people do not receive proper financial education.

CLASSIFICATION OF ETFS
CHAPTER 15

Before looking at practical elements by learning how to build a portfolio of ETFs depending on your goal, I would like to show you a classification of ETFs based on the benchmark that the basket of securities goes to replicate. Typically, they are distinguished into:

Monetary. They do not constitute a true and proper instrument of investment but arise from the need to manage the liquidity present in your account. They characteristically manage a basket of short/very short-term bonds, usually 12 months or less.

The investment isn't the purpose, but rather guaranteeing a minimal remuneration for the liquidity that is firmly in your account, even if we are currently seeing interest rates at zero or nearly zero all over the world during this historical time, the yield of these ETFs is null if not entirely negative.

Bonds. They invest in bonds and allow for broad level diversification:

- Geographical (Europe, USA, emerging countries, etc.);
- Issuer (government securities, corporate);
- Maturity (short, medium, long term);
- Currency (Euro, Dollar, exchange rate hedging, etc.);
- Income (accumulation, distribution).

As you can see, each level can be further diversified.

The advantage offered by bond ETFs is that they enable you to invest small assets while efficiently diversifying your portfolio. However, as you have seen with bonds, a key concept remains the link between interest rates and the price of the individual bonds that make up an ETF's basket.

In 2021, this is not a factor to be underestimated, especially given the low level of interest rates. An increase in rates would lead to a drop in the price of individual bonds, and as a result, a depreciation of the ETF.

Equities. They are characterized by replicating a basket of stocks. They present numerous advantages:

- Low commissions. Since with a single transaction you can buy all the shares that make up the basket;
- Low risk. The purchase of an ETF compared to a single stock has undoubted advantages in terms of lower volatility and therefore lower risk.
- Diversification. As with bond ETFs, equity ETFs can also be diversified geographically (Europe, America, Asia, Emerging Countries, etc.), by sector (banks, industry, telecommunications, real estate, etc.), by theme (allowing you to invest in a specific theme which is generally environmental, social or energy-related), etc.

As you have already seen, individual stocks are certainly not an ideal investment as they require adequate knowledge of the company you intend to invest in, as well as experience, which most of you do not possess. ETFs are definitely a better alternative for investing in the stock market.

Structured. Structured ETFs deserve a separate mention. They are synthetically replicated ETFs which invest in a basket of derivative instruments (futures) and which allow the replication of complex strategies (which until a few years ago were the exclusive prerogative of hedge funds) or non-linear strategies respecting the trends concerning reference benchmarks.

The main types of structured ETFs are:

- <u>Short</u>. They allow the investor to take an opposite position to the benchmark. In concrete terms, these ETFs increase in value when the benchmark falls in price. They are therefore a way of speculating on the downside of financial markets.
- <u>Leveraged</u>. They allow the investor to realize an additional return (but also a loss) with respect to the benchmark. The additional return is determined by the leverage effect, which allows the performance of the benchmark to be amplified. For example, if the benchmark earns 1.5% today, a "3x leveraged ETF" earns 4.5% (1.5% x 3 = 4.5%). If tomorrow the benchmark achieves -2%, the same ETF will lose 6% (-2% x 3 = -6%).

They are therefore instruments that need to be treated with care and only by experienced people. Moreover, they are much more suitable for speculation (trading) than for investment. This is why I do not recommend the use of structured ETFs and why you won't find them mentioned again in this course.

In conclusion, you have seen how ETFs are very versatile tools that allow you to invest with low costs and low risks, even with little capital, diversifying in many ways and in different markets. It's the ideal tool for those who want to make an accumulation plan.

ETCs
Chapter 16

It often happens that ETCs are mistaken for ETFs, I too made this mistake initially. In reality, they have very different characteristics. ETCs, which stands for Exchange Traded Commodities, are characterised by not having an expiry date and, like ETFs, they passively replicate a benchmark whilst being listed on a regulated market.

But compared to ETFs, they are characterised by a greater choice of benchmarks and the absence of a tracking error since it is the issuer itself that guarantees the perfect performance of the reference benchmark.

ETCs differ from ETFs in that they are a debt instrument and therefore do not provide for segregation of assets, which means that the investor, in the event of default of the issuer, is exposed to the risk of insolvency and therefore to the loss of the amount invested. This difference means that ETCs carry a higher degree of risk than ETFs. For this reason, the investor should periodically check the rating, i.e., the assessment of the issuer's solvency.

However, some issuers deposit a monetary amount or securities in a separate account as collateral for investors.

Another critical issue with ETCs is the fact that the return is not only a function of the reference benchmark (and other factors that you will see later) but also depends on the issuer's rating. Simply put, if the issuer's strength declines, the price of the ETC will also tend to decline.

When choosing an ETC, you should consider two aspects:

- *replication of the reference benchmark*
- *the variables that influence the price*

Trying to be as clear and simple as possible I will explain these two aspects.

The **replication of the benchmark** can be:

- **Physical**. The money is used to directly buy the reference commodity (e.g., a precious metal such as gold, silver or platinum). ETCs belonging to this category usually contain the word "physical" in the name (for example Xtrackers Physical Gold ETC).
- **Synthetic**. When, due to storage problems, it is not possible to buy the raw material reference (think of cotton, calves or oil), the replication takes place through the purchase of futures contracts. The futures contract is a forward contract whereby parties undertake to exchange a certain asset (financial or real) at a fixed price and with a deferred settlement at a future date. In practice, by purchasing a futures contract, I undertake to buy the benchmark at maturity at a price already set.

In an ETC, the difference between the two methods is important and characterizes the price and efficiency of the ETC itself.

The variables that (eventually) influence the price of an ETC are different and depend on the type of replica of the reference benchmark.

<u>If the replication is physical</u>, there are two variables that affect the price: the price of the reference commodity and, possibly, the currency exchange rate. Since commodities are quoted in dollars, anyone who buys an ETC and is not a resident of the United States will have to be careful about the exchange rate of their country's currency against the U.S. dollar (for example, if a person lives in Germany, Eur-Usd, if he lives in Australia, Aud-Usd, if he lives in Canada Usd-Cad, etc.).

<u>If the replication is synthetic</u>, in addition to the two variables seen above, you must also take into account another aspect. Futures, being derivatives, have an expiration date. In proximity to the expiration the futures contract gets replaced with the successive one; what happens, in jargon terms, is called a rollover. Generally, on this occasion, there is a misalignment between the price of the ETC and the price of the commodity that can be to the advantage or disadvantage of the ETC (I'm not going to explain this process, it is too technical and complicated).

In conclusion, ETCs are a great way to further diversify your portfolio and protect it in the event of a downturn. However, you need to be careful about what you buy. ETCs with synthetic replication are inefficient and you need some experience to use them properly, otherwise, you risk heavy losses. Therefore, they are unsuitable for those who want to invest their savings in the long term (they are more suitable for experienced traders than for quiet investors).

Personally, as an experienced trader in commodities, I only use in my investments ETCs that physically replicate a commodity. This is for several reasons that would be too complicated to explain. I do, from time to time, add ETCs that replicate a basket of commodities but only for hedging purposes (which are however unsuitable for inexperienced investors) and then, only for short periods.

Just for the record, and to complete this topic, in the panorama of ETPs there are also some ETNs that replicate some currency pairs (such as Eur-Usd). They are instruments that allow you to position yourself upwards on a currency (for example the U.S. dollar) and downward on another (the Euro).

In theory, these would be ideal as hedges of foreign currency instruments but in practice, they are not very liquid and not traded a lot, therefore they are not ideal to include in a portfolio.

A TALK ON FINANCIAL EDUCATION

CRITERIA FOR CHOOSING ETFs AND ETCs
CHAPTER 17

You have begun to familiarize yourself with this financial instrument that lends itself very well to long-term investments. Now it's time to get more practical by seeing how you can select ETFs and ETCs.

The selection of ETFs is very important and requires care and attention. It is a step-by-step process that begins with an analysis of each product's characteristics and ends with identifying the most efficient ones to meet your financial objective.

Choosing ETFs has two processes:

- **<u>Objective</u>**, the analysis of the characteristics and data of each ETF.
- **<u>Subjective</u>**, the investor's financial planning, which includes the financial objective, time perspective and degree of risk.

Let's see what steps you need to take care of when choosing an ETF.

1. **<u>Select and classify ETFs divided by class</u>**: monetary, equity, bond. As mentioned, structured ETFs are not suitable for investment so you must therefore leave them alone.

2. **Analyse the stocks or bonds that make up the basket of each ETF.** You basically have to verify that the ETF is in line with your investment idea. Now, a clarification. It's not that you have to analyse all ETFs on the market one by one, but only those related to the benchmark you want to invest in. For example, if you are not interested in investing in the emerging bond market, you will ignore all ETFs that are composed of bonds issued in that specific geographic sector.

There are so many issuing companies and consequently so many ETFs on the same benchmark. You have to choose the one that best represents what you want to invest in. For example, if you want to buy an ETF with shares from Asian countries but you don't want Chinese securities, maybe because the Evergrande case scares you, you have to look, among all the ETFs, for one whose basket is composed of shares from Asian countries but without Chinese securities.

In addition, you need to check that the ETF basket is actually diversified and there is no skewing towards a particular area. Let me give you another example. Some ETFs replicate the world stock market, so with stocks from a bit of all five continents. However, there are ETFs with baskets composed of 35-40% from American Stocks and others in which the percentage is double. Understand that if your goal is to maximally diversify your equity investment, an ETF composed of 80% U.S. stocks is not for you.

My advice is not to base your choice on performance as ETFs on the same benchmark but with differently composed baskets can give very different results. Always base your decisions on your own investment idea.

3. **Your degree of risk**. If you are a very prudent investor, then your choice must fall on physically replicated ETFs, so you can avoid having to insert into your portfolio synthetically replicated ETFs that are a bit riskier unless there are no alternatives (i.e., there are no physically replicated ETFs of a specific benchmark on the market, such as in African countries' equities). I also personally prefer physically replicated ETFs, but not everyone is the same.
4. **Check how much the currency exchange rate affects you**, if at all. You will need to distinguish between:
    - Currency of the asset, i.e., the currency of the stocks or bonds that make up the ETF basket;
    - Currency of denomination, the currency in which the ETF was issued;
    - Trading currency, the currency in which the ETF is traded (e.g., in Euro if listed on the Frankfurt Stock Exchange or in dollars if listed on the New York Stock Exchange).

This is an aspect you should not underestimate. For example, for me, because I am Italian, even if an ETF on the index S&P 500 is quoted on the Stock Exchange of Milan or Frankfurt, and therefore in Euro, the Stocks inside are in the American currency (dollars). So, the Eur-Usd exchange rate will affect the performance of the ETF anyway (either positively or negatively).

To overcome this variable, the saver who wishes to invest in ETFs listed in a foreign currency but without the exchange rate risk can opt for a hedged ETF. A hedged ETF contains an internal mechanism, realised through derivative contracts, which eliminates the exchange rate risk. However, this hedging of the exchange rate risk has a cost that will affect the price of the ETF.

5. **Dividends**. Not all, but many ETFs issue dividends (as if they were a common stock), based on the dividends issued by the securities within it. These can be:
    - distributed. On the ex-dividend day, the portion of the dividend is subtracted from the ETF price and on the payment day credited into the investor's account (multiplied by the number of units the investor holds in his portfolio).
    - accumulated. Dividends are not distributed but accumulated within the price, increasing the price of the ETF.

    The choice is up to you. If you need an income to meet some expenses or to spend as you see fit, then you should choose ETFs that distribute dividends. If, on the other hand, you don't need an extra income in your account, it's much better to go for ETFs that accumulate dividends because, as explained through compound interest, they perform better in the long run than distributors.

6. Another important factor in your decision making is **liquidity**, i.e., whether it is a heavily traded ETF. An ETF is defined as liquid when trades are high and supply and demand are not problematic or anomalous. Conversely, if an ETF is illiquid, it means that not many trades occur and supply and demand are far apart. This leads to difficulties when you want to sell an ETF and often being forced to do so at a very disadvantageous price.

    The liquidity of an ETF can depend on several factors:
    - Liquidity of the benchmark. The formula is simple: the more liquid and traded the benchmark is, the more liquid the ETF will also be.
    - Capitalisation of the ETF. Again, the relationship is very clear: the greater the money supply (i.e., the

total savings of all investors) managed, the greater the liquidity of the ETF.
- Life of the ETF. Simply put, how many years an ETF has been listed. ETFs that have been listed for longer tend to be more liquid and traded. Probably due to the fact that being longer on the markets, they tend to be more trusted by investors. Certainly, the broader the time series (i.e., the past years' performance) to be analysed, the more accurate the performance analysis will be.
- Listing market. That is the market where the ETF is listed and traded. Some ETFs are listed on multiple exchanges. Your choice should fall on the one that is most heavily traded. This, however, also depends on the bank or broker you make your investments with.

In conclusion, you only need to invest in liquid ETFs, so that, in case you need to divest, you will have no problem doing so. How to decide if an ETF is heavily or thinly traded? Generally, look at the daily countervalue (given by the price of the ETF multiplied by the number of units traded in a day) and in my opinion this should be at least 600-700 thousand dollars.

7. **Costs**. A cost that few investors take into consideration is the percentage difference between the bid (the best available price for purchase) and ask (the best available price for sale), between ETFs that invest in the same benchmark. This, as you have seen, depends very much on the liquidity of the ETF but it isn't the only thing. Also, volatility in a given historical moment can contribute to widening the bid/ask range. The wider the bid/ask percentage difference, the more this will negatively affect the ETF performance.

One figure you should pay attention to is the TER (Total Expenses Ratio), an indicator that allows you to calculate the annual cost of the ETF. The TER includes all of the ETF's administrative, marketing and legal expenses. Like all costs, the TER affects the performance of the ETF, so you should choose an ETF with a low TER.

The sum of the bid/ask percentage difference and the TER gives you the total cost of an ETF.

Choosing an ETC is pretty much the same as choosing an ETF, it just differs in a couple of ways:

- **Issuer;**
- **Replication type**.

The issuers of ETCs are at risk of default, therefore, it is important to check their reliability. Without getting too confused with the analysis of financial statements, just check a couple of aspects: the possible rating of a specialised company and the trend of the share of the company. If the issuer has received a bad rating or the title is collapsing, it is a good idea to investigate why.

The type of replication in ETCs is even more important than in ETFs. I do not recommend synthetic replication; physical replicas are much quieter and more suitable for long-term investments. I prefer physical replication in ETFs, even more so in ETCs.

If you are unclear about something, don't worry. I will now show you some examples of how I choose an ETF to better clarify the process.

A TALK ON FINANCIAL EDUCATION

How to choose an ETF, example 1

Chapter 18

So, you have seen the many elements that you need to evaluate when researching a particular ETF. At this point, most of you will find it all very complicated, without having the slightest idea of where to go to do such research.

This is to be expected, at least initially. Researching an ETF is a long process that requires patience and a lot of attention. After all, you are looking for a financial instrument through which to invest your savings (and I assume you care about your savings).

When you go to buy a pair of shoes, for example, I don't think you go into the store, grab the first box you find and after paying, go home satisfied. You choose the model, the colour, the size, you try them on to feel how they fit on your feet... in short, you dedicate the necessary time to the purchase. The same goes for choosing the right ETF or ETFs for your investment idea.

However, on the internet, there are several screeners (literally, sifters) that can help you in your search for ETFs and that allow you to select different parameters. However, I must point something out here.

Currently, for those who live outside the United

States, it is not possible to buy ETFs listed in New York (at least not most of them). Therefore, trying to make a search using an American screener (like etf.com or etfdb.com) is totally useless, because it has a database of only American ETFs which you cannot buy.

You need to use a screener that searches through all ETFs listed in Europe (London, Frankfurt, Amsterdam, Milan, etc). I will now show you an example of what you need to do. I will use the screener from **JustETF** (https://www.justetf.com/it/find-etf.html). On this site, on the left, you can select the parameters (out of the available ones).

Important! In "ETF Listing" you have to click on "**Show all listings**" so that you can see all listed ETFs in the results, otherwise, the screener will limit the search to the default exchange, i.e., the London Exchange (figure 4).

Figure 4 - Exchange Selection (JustETF.com)

Let's say my goal is to invest in the US stock market whilst diversifying. So, I want an ETF that is heavily traded (liquid), with physical replication, low TER, no currency exchange issues, accumulates dividends and has a longevity of at least 5 years.

I proceed with my research (figure 5).

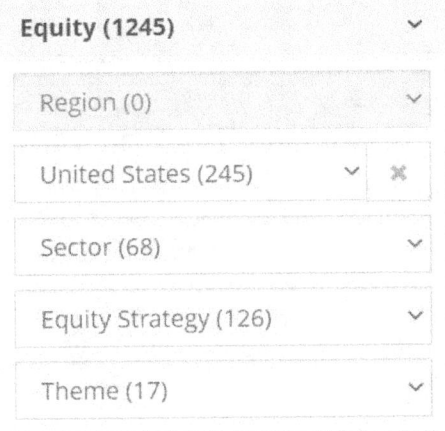

Figure 5 - Screener (JustETF.com)

You can't select all the variables but it's not a big deal, the search will just take a little longer. I have selected as a geographical area the United States. I want an ETF that is similar to SPY which, because it is listed on the New York Stock Exchange, I can't buy it as an Italian citizen and since I don't want to worry about the exchange rate, my choice has to be in Euros (EUR) or Euro hedged. EUR Hedged means, as you have seen before, that the ETF contains within it a mechanism, realized through derivative contracts, that cancels the exchange rate risk.

The other characteristics I am looking for are: a well-capitalized ETF (so liquid), that has physical replication, low costs (so a maximum TER of 0.20%), that accumulates dividends and that has been listed for at least 5 years.

In figure 6 is the result of my research.

With only the choice of the United States, the search returns 245 ETFs. I personally prefer to go and look at the various ETFs myself, not making the screener do it for me, but this is a personal choice.

A TALK ON FINANCIAL EDUCATION

Fund Name	Chart 4 Weeks	Fund CCY	Fund Size (in m €)	TER in % p.a.	1Y in %
BNP Paribas Equity Low Vol US					
BNP Paribas Easy Equity Low Volatility US UCITS ETF		EUR	11	0.30%	24.84%
BVP Nasdaq Emerging Cloud					
WisdomTree Cloud Computing UCITS ETF USD Acc		USD	604	0.40%	45.68%
BofA Merrill Lynch Diversified Core Plus Fixed Rate Preferred Securities (CHF Hedged)					
Invesco Preferred Shares UCITS UCITS ETF CHF Hedged		CHF Hedged	1	0.55%	5.28%
BofA Merrill Lynch Diversified Core Plus Fixed Rate Preferred Securities (EUR Hedged)					
Invesco Preferred Shares UCITS UCITS ETF EUR Hedged		EUR Hedged	27	0.55%	5.26%
Capital Strength					
First Trust Capital Strength UCITS ETF Acc		USD	11	0.60%	29.20%

Figure 6 - Search results (JustETF.com)

What I need to do next is click on "Fund Size (in m €)" to put the ETFs in order of capitalisation (figure 7).

Fund Name	Chart 4 Weeks	Fund CCY	Fund Size (in m €)	TER in % p.a.	1Y in %
iShares Core S&P 500 UCITS ETF (Acc)		USD	46,726	0.07%	39.44%
Vanguard S&P 500 UCITS ETF		USD	28,119	0.07%	39.43%
iShares Core S&P 500 UCITS ETF USD (Dist)		USD	12,211	0.07%	39.45%
Invesco S&P 500 UCITS ETF		USD	10,131	0.05%	39.51%
Xtrackers S&P 500 Swap UCITS ETF 1C		USD	8,115	0.15%	39.75%
iShares Nasdaq 100 UCITS ETF (Acc)		USD	7,013	0.33%	39.30%
iShares MSCI USA SRI UCITS ETF USD (Acc)		USD	6,756	0.20%	40.70%
Xtrackers MSCI USA UCITS ETF 1C		USD	5,542	0.07%	39.87%
HSBC S&P 500 UCITS ETF USD		USD	5,024	0.09%	39.12%
SPDR S&P 500 UCITS ETF		USD	4,968	0.09%	39.37%
iShares S&P 500 EUR Hedged UCITS ETF (Acc)		EUR Hedged	4,734	0.20%	35.02%

Figure 7 - ETFs in order of capitalisation (JustETF.com)

Now, given the number of ETFs there are, I have to select all of the ones with a capitalization of at least 1 billion and that are EUR or EUR hedged. This reduces the list to just 8 ETFs:

- iShares S&P 500 EUR Hedged UCITS ETF (Acc)
- Amundi Index MSCI USA SRI UCITS ETF DR (C)
- Lyxor S&P 500 UCITS ETF - Dist (EUR)
- Amundi S&P 500 UCITS ETF EUR (C)
- Amundi S&P 500 UCITS ETF Daily Hedged EUR (C)
- Lyxor Nasdaq-100 UCITS ETF - Acc
- BNP Paribas Easy S&P 500 UCITS ETF EUR
- UBS ETF (IE) MSCI USA hedged EUR UCITS ETF (EUR) A-acc

My selection is not finished yet, I need to check the other parameters. To do this I click on the name of each ETF. From the list above I discard Lyxor Nasdaq-100 UCITS ETF - Acc because it replicates the performance of Nasdaq 100 stocks (another American stock market index).

I'm also eliminating Lyxor S&P 500 UCITS ETF - Dist (EUR) because it has both synthetic replication and dividend distribution. Also eliminated are Amundi S&P 500 UCITS ETF EUR (C), Amundi S&P 500 UCITS ETF Daily Hedged EUR (C) and BNP Paribas Easy S&P 500 UCITS ETF EUR which have synthetic replication.

The list has already been whittled down to three ETFs:

- iShares S&P 500 EUR Hedged UCITS ETF (Acc)
- Amundi Index MSCI USA SRI UCITS ETF DR (C)
- UBS ETF (IE) MSCI USA hedged EUR UCITS ETF (EUR) A-acc

All three have a very similar TER, Amundi 0.18%, UBS 0.19% and iShares 0.20%. The last parameter is longevity.

UBS ETF (IE) MSCI USA hedged EUR UCITS ETF (EUR) A-acc is eliminated having been on the market for just over 2 years (June 2019). So is Amundi Index MSCI USA SRI UCITS ETF DR (C) which has longevity of three years (September 2018).

So, my choice falls on iShares S&P 500 EUR Hedged UCITS ETF (Acc) which has all the features I'm looking for (and also, as an Italian, is listed on the Milan Stock Exchange).

As I have mentioned, by clicking on the names you can see all the most crucial features, such as the list of all the stocks that make up the ETF - although, in this case, it is not as useful to know the names (them being the 500 companies present in the S&P 500 index), as it is to know their weight within the basket - and the percentage of the individual sectors within the ETF. You can also download the fact sheet and the KIID.

Alternatively, just do a Google search of the ETF name and then go and look at the features directly on the issuing company's website (I personally do this).

So, you have seen an example of how you might choose the correct ETF for your investment idea. In this case on equities. Below I will show you two more examples, one for bonds and one for an ETC on gold.

A TALK ON FINANCIAL EDUCATION

How to choose an ETF, example 2
Chapter 19

In the previous example, you saw how I searched for an ETF that replicated the performance of the S&P 500 index and had all the features I wanted. It was all in all easy and fairly quick even though my search initially yielded a high number of results.

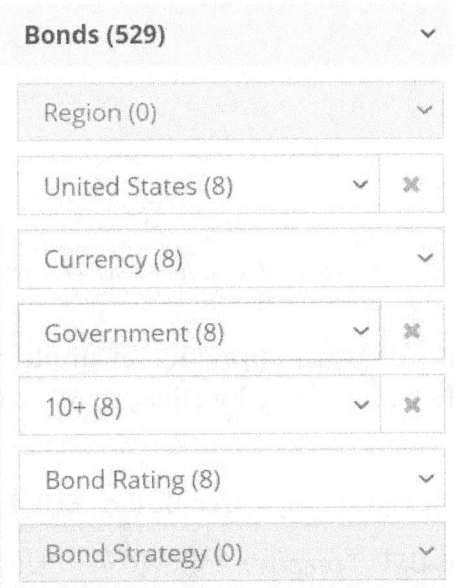

Figure 8 - Screener (JustETF.com)

I now want to include in my portfolio an ETF that

invests in the long-term (i.e., 10 years or more) with a US bond market that is liquid, on the market for at least 5 years, has no foreign exchange issues, has physical replication, distributes returns and is low cost. I arrange my search by selecting "United States", "Government" and "10+" as the duration (figure 8 above).

There are only 8 results, which makes my selection process a lot easier (figure 9).

Fund Name	Chart 4 Weeks	Fund CCY	Fund Size (in m €)	TER in % p.a.	1Y in %
Bloomberg US 10+ Year Treasury Bond					
Lyxor US Treasury 10+Y (DR) UCITS ETF - Acc		USD	2	0.07%	-
Lyxor US Treasury 10+Y (DR) UCITS ETF - Dist		USD	237	0.07%	-7.70%
SPDR Barclays 10+ Year US Treasury Bond UCITS ETF		USD	27	0.15%	-7.65%
Bloomberg US 10+ Year Treasury Bond (EUR Hedged)					
Lyxor US Treasury 10+Y (DR) UCITS ETF - Monthly Hedged to EUR - Dist		EUR Hedged	55	0.10%	-9.95%
UBS ETF (LU) Bloomberg US 10+ Year Treasury Bond UCITS ETF (hedged to EUR) A-dis		EUR Hedged	30	0.25%	-10.01%
ICE US Treasury 20+					
iShares USD Treasury Bond 20+yr UCITS ETF (Dist)		USD	842	0.07%	-7.78%

Figure 9 - Search results (JustETF.com)

Unlike in the previous example, this time I will arrange the ETFs by currency by clicking on "Fund CCY" (figure 10).

There are only three EUR or EUR hedged ETFs.

- iShares USD Treasury Bond 20+yr EUR Hedged UCITS
- Lyxor US Treasury 10+Y (DR) UCITS ETF - Monthly Hedged to EUR - Dist
- UBS ETF (LU) Bloomberg US 10+ Year Treasury Bond

UCITS ETF (hedged to EUR) A-dis

Fund Name	Chart 4 Weeks	Fund CCY	Fund Size (in m €)	TER in % p.a.	1Y in %
iShares USD Treasury Bond 20+yr EUR Hedged UCITS ETF		EUR Hedged	138	0.10%	-9.77%
Lyxor US Treasury 10+Y (DR) UCITS ETF - Monthly Hedged to EUR - Dist		EUR Hedged	55	0.10%	-9.95%
UBS ETF (LU) Bloomberg US 10+ Year Treasury Bond UCITS ETF (hedged to EUR) A-dis		EUR Hedged	30	0.25%	-10.01%
iShares USD Treasury Bond 20+yr UCITS ETF (Dist)		USD	842	0.07%	-7.78%
iShares USD Treasury Bond 20+yr UCITS ETF USD (Acc)		USD	217	0.07%	-7.78%
Lyxor US Treasury 10+Y (DR) UCITS ETF - Acc		USD	2	0.07%	-

Figure 10 - ETFs in order of currency (JustETF.com)

All three are not very well-capitalized, the highest being **iShares USD Treasury Bond 20+yr EUR Hedged UCITS** which is also the ETF my choice falls on. *UBS ETF (LU) Bloomberg US 10+ Year Treasury Bond UCITS ETF (hedged to EUR) A-dis* in addition to having a low capitalisation also has costs that amount to more than double the other two and *Lyxor US Treasury 10+Y (DR) UCITS ETF - Monthly Hedged to EUR - Dist* has also results, from previous years, that are underwhelming.

The iShares USD Treasury Bond 20+yr EUR Hedged UCITS ETF has been on the market for less than 5 years, exactly 4 years and 1 month at the moment. Although capitalisation is not large (only 138 mil.) the London Stock Exchange (LSE) listed ETF has high volumes and therefore does not seem to give liquidity problems.

As with the previous example, by clicking on the name you can see all the features such as the list of all the bonds that make up the ETF and their weight within the basket. You can also download the fact sheet and the KIID. Alternatively, as mentioned above, just do a Google search of the name of the ETF and then go and see the characteristics directly on the site of the issuing company.

So, you have seen how I chose an ETF on the US bond that respected my investment idea as much as possible. There will not always be an ETF or ETC that will have all the characteristics you are looking for. In that case, you either accept the closest one that has at least all the most important qualities, or you change investment type (and ETF).

A TALK ON FINANCIAL EDUCATION

How to choose an ETC, example 3

Chapter 20

In this third and last example, I will show you, very quickly, how you can choose an ETC, in this case on gold. The characteristics I'm looking for are kind of always the same. I want a liquid ETC, with physical replication, low costs, no foreign exchange issues and that has been on the market for at least 5 years.

Fund Name	Chart 4 Weeks	Fund CCY	Fund Size (in m €)	TER in % p.a.	1Y in %	
Gold						
☐ Amundi Physical Gold ETC (C)		USD	3,037	0.12%	-4.46%	○
☐ boerse.de Gold ETC		EUR	8	0.00%	-	○
☐ EUWAX Gold		EUR	439	0.00%	-4.17%	○
☐ EUWAX Gold II		EUR	794	0.00%	-4.50%	○
☐ Gold Bullion Securities		USD	3,119	0.40%	-4.70%	○
☐ GPF Physical Gold ETC		USD	14	0.12%	-	○
☐ HANetf The Royal Mint Physical Gold ETC Securities		USD	288	0.22%	-4.84%	○
☐ Invesco Physical Gold A		USD	11,378	0.15%	-4.62%	○
☐ iShares Physical Gold ETC		USD	10,836	0.15%	-4.45%	○
☐ WisdomTree Core Physical Gold		USD	132	0.15%	-	○
☐ WisdomTree Physical Gold		USD	5,053	0.39%	-4.69%	○
☐ WisdomTree Physical Swiss Gold		USD	2,939	0.15%	-4.46%	○

Figure 11 - Search results (JustETF.com)

In the screener of JustETF, I click on precious metals. This gives me the whole list of ETCs, starting from gold, up to silver and passing by palladium, platinum etc. (figure 11 above).

I have several ETFs to choose from. So, I click on "Fund Size (in m €)" to arrange them in order of size (figure 12).

Fund Name	Chart 4 Weeks	Fund CCY	Fund Size (in m €)	TER in % p.a.	1Y in %
Xetra-Gold		EUR	11,710	0.00%	-4.28%
Invesco Physical Gold A		USD	11,378	0.15%	-4.62%
iShares Physical Gold ETC		USD	10,836	0.15%	-4.45%
WisdomTree Physical Gold		USD	5,053	0.39%	-4.69%
Gold Bullion Securities		USD	3,119	0.40%	-4.70%
Amundi Physical Gold ETC (C)		USD	3,037	0.12%	-4.46%
WisdomTree Physical Swiss Gold		USD	2,939	0.15%	-4.46%
Xtrackers Physical Gold ETC (EUR)		USD	1,995	0.25%	-4.56%
WisdomTree Physical Silver		USD	1,979	0.49%	-1.86%
Xtrackers Physical Gold EUR Hedged ETC		EUR Hedged	1,898	0.59%	-7.77%
Xtrackers IE Physical Gold ETC Securities		USD	1,773	0.15%	-4.45%
Xtrackers Physical Silver ETC (EUR)		USD	862	0.40%	-0.31%
Xtrackers IE Physical Gold EUR Hedged ETC Securities		EUR Hedged	810	0.28%	-8.16%

Figure 12 - ETFs in order of capitalisation (JustETF.com)

The first, **Xetra-Gold** is the largest and most traded (so very liquid), in Euro, has no cost (of management, you still have to pay the commissions of the bank or broker), has a physical replica and has been on the market since November 2007.

All this, as in the previous examples, can be found by clicking on the name or going directly to see the characteristics of the ETF on the site of the issuing company.

At this point, choosing an ETF or ETC should seem less complicated to you even if you have to spend some time on it.

You have seen the criteria, explained in theory and then in practice, in the examples. To help you in your choice you can use the JustETF screener (https://www.justetf.com/it/find-etf.html), and, on the left, by selecting the parameters (those available) that interest you, reduce the number of results.

Clicking on each of the results, you can go and read the characteristics (or go and see them directly on the website of the issuing company). You can also download and read the fact sheet and the KIID (in PDF format).

If like me, you have an account with a broker that allows you to buy ETFs, chances are it already comes with a screener. No one is stopping you from using that (or another free screener), however, I have found that JustETF, for a European investor, is very well done.

A TALK ON FINANCIAL EDUCATION

CREATING A PORTFOLIO
CHAPTER 21

Before you even go looking for the ETF or ETFs to buy, you need to have the portfolio you want to build clearly set out in your mind. In constructing your portfolio, there are a few points that you need to be clear on, and I will explain these below.

Risk-Return Ratio. In my life, I have received the question, "how much do you earn with trading?" at least one hundred times. And the same question comes from those who wanted to invest, the first concern for them is how much they could earn. No one ever asked me about the losses or the risks I or them may face. The truth is that return and risk, gain and loss, are two sides of the same coin. If you are aiming for a bigger gain, then you are also taking a bigger risk.

Let me give you an example. Investing in a long-term US (treasury) bond ETF gives about a 2.5% return per year, investing in an HY (High Yield) bond ETF gives more than double that return, about 5.7%. The question is, which one would you invest in?

If you answered the second, your answer is wrong. If, on the other hand, you answered the first, the answer is... wrong. How can you decide to invest in something without knowing the risk you are going up against? Obviously, there is a reason why the two ETFs give such different annual returns. The first one is lower but has on its side the fact that it is composed of treasury bonds, so it has a high rating. In practice, losing your money would mean putting the U.S. in default, which is very unlikely (at least at the time I'm writing).

The second is composed of bonds issued by companies (mostly American), some of which have a low rating (defined as "junk") and are therefore decidedly less secure than treasury bonds. It is obvious that if a bond has a yield of 13% per year, it means that the company that issued it has a bad rating and there is the possibility that at maturity it will not be able to honour the debt.

So, the answer to the question is, "it depends on your investment priorities and the risk you are willing to take".

Efficiency. A key point is that you need to build your portfolio in the same way that a tailor would make your suit. It has to be tailored to you, to your investment idea, to your risk appetite, to your financial goal, to the duration you have envisioned. Only then can it be an efficient portfolio.

Don't think for a moment about asking me or anyone else to build you a portfolio to invest in. I would tailor it to me which would almost certainly not coincide with your investment idea. That would only bring you to worry and sleepless nights. And even if you do make a profit in the end, it can hardly be said that that portfolio is efficient for you.

Don't you find it at least a bit bizarre that this stressful approach means getting what you want to improve your quality of life but at the expense of making your quality of life worse?

So, follow the dictates of your investment idea and build your own portfolio. Only then can it be called efficient.

Diversify. This is a key concept when building a portfolio and it's a bit more complex than you've seen it so far. When you buy an ETF, you diversify your investment across multiple stocks or bonds. This is all fine and good, but diversification needs to happen at the portfolio level as well.

You must invest in several markets (equities, bonds, commodities...) which are not correlated with each other in such a way that the fall in one ETF is at least partly covered by the rise in another ETF. Two markets are correlated if a rise in one corresponds to a rise in the other and vice versa, a fall in one corresponds to a fall in the other. The two markets are not correlated if this relationship is broken.

Diversification is not something that increases the performance of your portfolio but decreases the risk.

An example can be found in so-called safe-haven assets. In periods of sharp declines in stock markets, it happens that large investors (funds) exit the stock market and invest in safe-haven assets, considered safer, especially gold. If you go and see, in 2008 in the face of a sharp fall in equity markets following the bankruptcy of Lehman Brothers, gold closed the year with a positive performance. It would not have been enough to cover the entire loss suffered by the stock market but nevertheless, it would have diminished its magnitude. The same happened in 2020.

A simple portfolio diversification is as follows:

- 25% monetary (i.e., short-term bonds, maximum three years);
- 25% long-term bond (10 years or more);
- 25% stock;
- 25% gold.

This way, you have a fairly balanced portfolio with low risks. Monetary and bonds do not only bring home a return but also lower the volatility of the portfolio. Equities are the riskiest part and the one that contributes the most to the performance of the portfolio. Gold mainly serves as a hedge.

Percentages can be changed depending on the historical period. If you are living in a profitable period for the stock, you can increase the exposure to the detriment of gold for example. In periods of uncertainty, you can do the exact opposite, decreasing the stock and increasing the other three.

Always keep in mind that choosing the markets you invest in and their percentages is what will determine the performance of your portfolio. You need to weigh the markets you invest in well, based on your financial objective.

Balancing. After seeing how you can diversify a portfolio the next step is balancing it. Unfortunately, this is easier said than done because you have to use your calculator. I'll explain it with an example, trying to make it as simple as possible on the numerical level.

You want to invest $ 100,000, divided into four equal parts (25%) for each asset just as seen above. So, $ 25,000 in cash, $ 25,000 in bonds, $ 25,000 in stocks and $ 25,000 in gold. All ETFs were purchased to provide for the accumulation of dividends/returns.

After one year, the monetary gained 2%, the bond gained 5%, the stock gained 22% and the ETC on gold lost 5%. Now the percentages into which the investment is divided are no longer all 25% but:

- monetary ($ 25,500) 24.06%.
- bond ($ 26,250) 24.76%.
- stocks ($ 30,500) 28.77%.

- gold ($ 23,750) 22.41

Therefore, the percentages have to be rebalanced to return to 25% again. First, you have to sum the value of all assets ($ 106,000) and divide by the number of assets (4): the result is $ 26,500. Then from the stock (the only asset of higher value), you have to disinvest $ 4,000 ($ 30,500 - $ 26,500 = $ 4,000) and distribute this money proportionally in the other assets.

So:

- monetary $ 1,000 ($ 25,500 + $ 1,000 = $ 26,500)
- bond $ 250 ($ 26,250 + $ 250 = $ 26,500)
- stocks $ 30,500 - $ 4,000 = $ 26,500
- gold $ 2,750 ($ 23,750 + $ 2,750 = $ 26,500)

The money you invested in cash, bonds and gold ($ 1,000 + $ 250 + $ 2,750 = $ 4,000) is exactly how much you disinvested from equities. Again, this is all very easy to say, but not so easy to do in practice, because you can't always disinvest and reinvest exactly what you have calculated. But you do have to try and get as close as possible.

The rebalancing can be done annually or semi-annually (I do not recommend shorter periods due to the costs involved in selling and buying ETFs). The same ETFs are regularly rebalanced by the issuing companies so that each stock or bond always maintains the same weight within the basket.

It is important, therefore, that you rebalance your portfolio from time to time because this will ensure it will always be well-diversified according to your investment idea and the financial objective you are pursuing. Otherwise, you will be more on one asset and less on others, changing the overall risk of the investment (and making the portfolio less efficient).

Some portfolio types
Chapter 22

Well, we have arrived at the final act of this guide, let's conclude with some types of portfolios. When building a portfolio, you must first establish the investment objective. You have to ask yourself, why am I investing this money? What do I want to achieve? How do I want to achieve it? Over how long a period of time? These answers will determine which choice of ETFs and/or ETCs you will invest in, since you have seen that ETFs, even with the same benchmark, may have different characteristics.

Obviously, they must be attainable objectives. Investing a thousand euros and hoping to make a million in 10 years is not feasible. Generally, those who invest do so to protect their savings from inflation, to have an annual (or six-monthly) income, or to supplement their pension when they reach the required age. These are all objectives that require different portfolios.

Next, you need to establish the time frame, i.e., how soon you want to achieve your goal. This depends not only on your age but also on the savings available to you.

Finally, you have to decide the risk you are willing to accept to achieve the goal, i.e., your risk appetite. As mentioned, greater gain also means greater risk. Investing in High Yield bonds allows you to earn more than doing so in U.S.

government bonds, but the risk of default by an issuer is also higher.

Risk appetite can be translated as your tolerance to fluctuations, even sharp ones in some cases, in the financial products you hold in your portfolio. You must quantify this risk and only choose the financial instruments that allow you to respect this parameter.

You need to evaluate everything well. If a goal is only achievable in the face of raising the risk beyond your tolerance threshold, then perhaps you should review your priorities and veer towards something quieter and easier to achieve. Also wrong is increasing the size of your investment to achieve your goal. The savings you invest should not be used for day-to-day expenses and their momentary deprivation should not cause you problems.

Now it is time to look at <u>investment strategies</u> depending on what the goal you wish to achieve is. First, there is a distinction to be made about portfolio management. Your portfolio can be managed:

- *passively*
- *actively*

What's the difference? <u>Managing a portfolio passively</u> means buying ETFs and leaving them in the portfolio without making any changes for the duration of the investment. This has the virtue that you don't have to spend time on them, at most a few hours a year, and the costs are ultimately almost negligible. However, keeping the same products in your portfolio at all times leaves it at the mercy of market fluctuations during periods of turbulence.

<u>Actively managing a portfolio</u> means buying and selling ETFs periodically as conditions change. It is immediately

obvious that such management requires a lot more time dedicated to it, the costs increase due to the higher number of commissions paid for purchases and sales and it also requires a certain knowledge of the dynamics of the markets. The advantage is that you can modify your portfolio as economic and market conditions change. This translates into a higher performance with a decrease in volatility and, consequently, risk.

Regardless of which management you choose, you must respect your investment objectives and not get emotional, especially during turbulent market times. Everything goes well when the markets go up, the problems come when the markets go down. Too many investors panic and sell for fear of losing their savings, losing sight of the objective and time perspective.

I remember in 2008 when someone wrote to me saying they had invested in BTPs (Italian government bonds) and was worried about losing everything (or almost everything) because of the financial crisis and the collapse of the stock market. This happens when you don't have a minimum knowledge of financial education.

Now, briefly, as this journey is not a solicitation to invest, I will show you three types of portfolios based on different needs.

Guaranteed Capital Portfolio. It is a strategy used by many banks to ask for higher commissions. It consists of buying a zero-coupon bond and, with the difference between nominal value and market price, buying one or more ETFs. In the worst cases, this will mean you will receive the entire capital invested at maturity. For the sake of clarity, I will show you an example.

I invest € 10,000. I buy the XYX zero-coupon bond at 88.50 for an outlay of € 8,850 and with my available savings (€ 1,150) I buy an ETF. At maturity, the bond will return me € 10,000 (all my capital); the ETF will represent my gain.

It is a type of conservative investment, that has the purpose of conserving capital whilst revaluating it. In this way, the risk is zeroed (not really, there is always a risk, even if minor, of the issuer, defaulting) and on top of that, you have a gain, even if this gain is low. It is an optimal alternative to leaving the firm savings on your current account annually eroded from inflation.

Periodic Annuity Portfolio. Expenses: we all have them. Mortgage or rent to pay, children's school, medical or life insurance, etc. So, it wouldn't hurt to get a periodic annuity (usually semi-annual or annual) to alleviate costs.

First, you have to choose ETFs that distribute returns (and not accumulate them). Then, to create this type of portfolio you have two options:

- *stocks*
- *bonds*

You have to choose whether to use ETFs on the stock markets or the bond markets. There is a difference, which I will now elucidate. Of the two, it is generally the equity that distributes a higher return. However, stocks are less regular and more volatile and therefore subject to declines (even strong declines in some cases as has happened in the past). If in the long term, they do not you're your investment any problems, they can however give you issues on dividends. Both because the year could close at a loss for a company, and because even though a gain has been achieved, the company may decide not to distribute dividends to shareholders (in practice, choosing not to distribute for that year but rather to accumulate).

Bonds, instead, are far calmer and more constant, without such great swings and, on top of this, are a lot less volatile than stocks and therefore more indicated for those who need a regular income coming in every six or twelve months. In my opinion, therefore, bond ETFs are to be preferred.

The second and final step concerns the choice of ETF. You have to choose a "*high yield*" ETF, which, all other conditions being equal (liquidity, physical or synthetic replication, currency, etc.) has the highest yield (dividend yield) (JustETF screener can help you make your choice).

Therefore, this type of portfolio is ideal for those who need to obtain a periodic income with an optical of the medium-long period. Moreover, it is low risk, being constructed entirely out of bonds (even if they are high-yield).

Retirement Portfolio. Whatever country you live in, it is well known that once you retire, what you receive each month will be less than your salary. You will be forced to use your savings to maintain your standard of living. This is a common concern for many people.

To get around this problem there are pension funds, whose main purpose is pension supplementation, or, much more simply, using accumulation ETFs.

The strategy that I adopt is the Accumulation Plan (but it is not the only one available). It consists of not investing all your savings immediately but rather breaking them up into monthly purchases or however regularly you wish (quarterly, six-monthly, annual).

This strategy is also great for people who do not have the capital to invest but who are able to save every month and put those savings into an accumulation plan, particularly young people. This is a subject that is very close to my heart, young people. They have two great allies in this strategy: lots of time in front of them and compound interest. Even with a little each month, a 25-year-old can secure a financially sound future.

Your age should decide which ETF to buy. If you still have many years before retiring, then the best strategy is to invest in an equity ETF (on world or U.S. equities) that guarantees better performance in the long run. If, on the other hand, you only have a few years left before retirement, then it is wiser to invest in a bond ETF (also global or U.S.) that is more conservative and less volatile.

The accumulation plan is very simple to implement, it does not require any special knowledge. It does not require time, at most a couple of hours per month. It solves the question of whether now is the right time to buy since purchases over time will give you an acceptable average price. You can customize it to your liking.

These are just three types of portfolios but there are many more. It's up to you now, if you are interested, to delve into this topic and build the one that best suits your needs.

Conclusion of the Financial Journey

Chapter 23

As I have specified, this is not really intended as a course, but rather a path that in a simple and clear way aims to improve your relationship with money and gives you a correct knowledge of the financial markets that are too often seen as negative and that instead represent the best way to make your savings return.

If you want to improve your financial situation, you have two options: hope to win the lottery or get busy. Here's a way to start saving. Not easy, perhaps, requiring sacrifices, definitely, but ask yourself this question: how much I really want to change my life for the better?

The day that changed my life, and I kid you not, was when I first kept a household budget. Seeing how much money I was futilely spending opened my eyes and made me realize that I needed to change my mindset. I began to give up some small things and save that money.

My goal was to become financially independent, that money would work for me and not the other way around. This took time, perseverance, determination but today I can say that I have achieved my goal. I am 51 years old; I am a successful trader (if I may be allowed a touch of arrogance) but not only that. I have three other activities that give me a passive income every month in addition to my accumulation plan that in ten years will allow me to retire and enjoy life to the fullest.

And I started from scratch. My family was far from rich. The only salary was that of my father, a simple worker, who had to support me, my two brothers and my mother. The word "save" was not in our vocabulary.

So, don't make excuses, they don't work. Do not put this off, do not procrastinate. And I am especially addressing young people who have many years ahead of them and, alas, an uncertain future. There is no limit to savings, you can start even with 20 or 50 euros per month. Starting an accumulation plan when you are young, even with such a low amount, will give you great benefits in the future.

I created this path with the sole purpose of helping as many people as possible improve their financial situation. And you can test the benefits right away by simply keeping a household budget. Over time, seeing your savings grow will give you a feeling of satisfaction and greater peace of mind. The knowledge that you have done the right things will strengthen the change in your mindset and increase your self-esteem. It will bring greater peace of mind to your family.

It is also important that if you have debts, you can pay them off and quickly. Debts are a source of worry and often of family problems. It is not always easy to get rid of them, but you can contact the debtor and agree on a monthly repayment. If they are reasonable people, they will understand your situation and agree to help you.

You must use a portion of your income to honour the agreements made. "Make sacrifices today for a more peaceful

A TALK ON FINANCIAL EDUCATION

life tomorrow." This is the motto that should accompany you at this stage.

So, I urge you to put into practice some of the aspects you have seen on this journey and to delve into greater depth on the topics covered. Along the way, I have mentioned some books that I recommend you read. On ETFs, there are many texts in all languages. Two other books I recommend you read are Ray Dalio's "**Principles: Life and Work**" and Burton G. Malkiel's "**A Random Walk Down Wall Street**".

If you have read this far, it means that what you have learned has intrigued you at least. Now, you have to take the first step, but you are not alone. If you have any questions, you can contact me as always by filling in the form on the page "Contact David", I will be happy to help you along, using what are my knowledge and experience. Or explaining concepts that are not yet clear to you.

www.ingramcontent.com/pod-product-compliance
Lightning Source LLC
Chambersburg PA
CBHW050245220526
45465CB00002B/555